HACKING WITH KALI LINUX

LINUX

Advanced Techniques and Strategies

Ryan Campbell

Table of Contents

INTRODUCTION

Welcome to a realm where cybersecurity is not just a shield but a powerful sword, where the mastery of advanced ethical hacking takes center stage. In this book, we invite you to step into the secret world of digital guardians, where the conventional rules of engagement no longer apply. It's a journey into the heart of cyber warfare, where you'll not only learn how to defend but also discover the exhilarating art of ethical hacking.

Are you ready to delve into the depths of modern security, where Kali Linux is your trusty companion? This book is your key to unlock the vault of advanced techniques and strategies that seasoned professionals use to safeguard and explore the digital landscape.

Whether you're a curious beginner, an experienced cybersecurity enthusiast, or someone seeking a thrilling career in ethical hacking, this book promises an adventure like no other. It's your passport to becoming a digital hero and a sentinel of the virtual realm. So, fasten your seatbelt, because the world of advanced ethical hacking awaits, and you're about to embark on a journey that will redefine the way you see the digital universe.

SETTING THE STAGE: THE POWER OF KALI LINUX

In the ever-evolving landscape of cybersecurity, where digital threats loom large, one name stands out as the ultimate weapon in the hands of ethical hackers – Kali Linux. This operating system, specifically designed for penetration testing, network assessments, and digital forensics, is your gateway to the world of advanced ethical hacking.

The Genesis of Kali Linux

To understand the power of Kali Linux, it's essential to explore its origins. Kali Linux, formerly known as BackTrack, emerged from the fusion of two prominent security-focused Linux distributions. The journey began with the release of BackTrack, which was revered by the security community for its extensive tools and ease of use. However, it was not without its challenges, and the need for a more refined and powerful platform became apparent.

In 2013, Kali Linux was introduced by Offensive Security, a leading organization in the field of cybersecurity training and certification. This marked a significant evolution in the realm of penetration testing and ethical hacking tools. Kali Linux was meticulously crafted, based on the Debian operating system, and designed with a singular purpose – to provide a robust and comprehensive environment for security professionals.

The Arsenal of Ethical Hackers

Kali Linux is often referred to as the "arsenal of ethical hackers" for a good reason. It houses an expansive array of pre-installed tools, each meticulously chosen to cater to various aspects of ethical hacking and penetration testing. Whether you're an aspiring ethical hacker, a seasoned cybersecurity expert, or even a digital enthusiast with a penchant for exploring the depths of cybersecurity, Kali Linux offers something for everyone.

Comprehensive Toolkit

One of the distinguishing features of Kali Linux is its comprehensive toolkit. It's a repository of over 600 tools, ranging from vulnerability assessment, network scanning, and information gathering to password cracking, wireless attacks, and digital forensics. The availability of this wide range of tools ensures that you're equipped to handle diverse scenarios and security challenges. You won't need to scramble for different software packages or tools; Kali Linux has already done the legwork for you.

Regular Updates

The power of Kali Linux doesn't stop with its extensive toolkit. What truly sets it apart is its commitment to staying current and relevant. The Kali Linux team maintains a rigorous update schedule, ensuring that tools are kept up to date and new ones are added as they become available. This dedication to continuous improvement guarantees that you're working with the latest and most effective tools, which is crucial in the ever-changing field of cybersecurity.

User-Friendly Interface

While the technical capabilities of Kali Linux are impressive, it's equally renowned for its user-friendly interface. Navigating the platform is straightforward, making it accessible to individuals at various skill levels. Whether you're a newcomer or a seasoned professional, you'll find that Kali Linux streamlines the process of setting up, configuring, and executing security assessments, allowing you to focus on the task at hand.

KALI LINUX AND ETHICAL HACKING

Kali Linux isn't just another operating system; it's the very foundation on which ethical hacking and penetration testing thrive. The power it offers lies not only in its technical capabilities but in the philosophy that underpins its existence. Kali Linux empowers users to employ their knowledge and skills responsibly, adhering to ethical guidelines and best practices.

A Platform for Learning

For those who aspire to become ethical hackers, Kali Linux is more than just a tool; it's a platform for learning and growth. It provides a controlled environment for honing your skills and gaining hands-on experience in a safe and legal manner. As you delve into the world of Kali Linux, you're not merely using tools; you're developing a profound understanding of cybersecurity, vulnerabilities, and their mitigations.

The Ethical Hacker's Ally

In the realm of ethical hacking, Kali Linux is your closest ally. It equips you to uncover weaknesses, assess risks, and bolster security. From discovering vulnerabilities in your own systems to testing the defenses of organizations and individuals who seek your expertise, Kali Linux is the linchpin that ensures you're well-prepared for the challenges ahead.

The Gateway to Advanced Ethical Hacking

In the world of cybersecurity, Kali Linux is more than an operating system; it's a symbol of empowerment. It provides you with the tools, knowledge, and environment needed to navigate the intricate web of digital security. As you embark on your journey through this book, you'll come to understand why Kali Linux is the go-to platform for ethical hackers and how it sets the stage for advanced techniques and strategies that will shape your path to becoming a proficient digital guardian.

Prepare to unlock the full potential of Kali Linux and harness its power to protect, explore, and excel in the domain of cybersecurity. Your adventure in the world of advanced ethical hacking begins here.

CHAPTER 1: MASTERING KALI LINUX

Unleashing the Full Potential of Kali Linux

In the world of ethical hacking and cybersecurity, Kali Linux stands as a beacon of knowledge, and its extensive toolkit is the arsenal of choice for digital warriors. As we delve into this chapter, we'll unlock the full potential of Kali Linux, which is more than just an operating system; it's your command center for navigating the intricate landscapes of cybersecurity.

The Power of Knowledge and Tools

Before we venture further, let's establish why knowledge and tools are the pillars of success in the realm of ethical hacking. Imagine you're a locksmith trying to secure a building. Your knowledge of different lock types, their vulnerabilities, and how to pick them is your knowledge base. The tools in your toolbox, like lock picks, tension wrenches, and bump keys, are your instruments of choice. With knowledge and tools in hand, you can effectively secure or breach locks as needed.

Similarly, in ethical hacking, knowledge equips you with a deep understanding of systems and networks. Tools are the means by which you probe and secure these digital fortresses. To be successful, you need both.

THE ROLE OF KALI LINUX

Now, consider Kali Linux as your virtual locksmith shop, complete with all the tools and knowledge needed to explore, protect, and conquer the digital realm. Let's break down the significance of Kali Linux:

1. Comprehensive Toolkit

Kali Linux houses an extensive toolkit comprising over 600 pre-installed tools. These tools cover a wide range of functions, including vulnerability analysis, network scanning, penetration testing, forensics, and much more. For example, the tool 'Nmap' allows you to scan networks and discover open ports and services, while 'Wireshark' is a packet analyzer used to inspect data on a network.

2. User-Friendly Interface

Kali Linux is renowned for its user-friendly interface. Whether you're a novice or an experienced cybersecurity professional, it offers a straightforward and intuitive platform for your operations. For instance, to conduct a network scan, you don't need to be a command-line wizard; tools like 'Zenmap' provide a graphical user interface for such tasks.

3. Diverse Use Cases

Kali Linux isn't confined to a single purpose. It serves a multitude of use cases. For example, it's an ideal environment for conducting penetration tests to identify vulnerabilities in systems. It also excels in digital forensics, helping investigators uncover digital evidence in legal cases.

4. Regular Updates

In the fast-paced world of cybersecurity, staying current is crucial. Kali Linux doesn't rest on its laurels; it follows a strict update schedule to ensure its tools are always up to date and effective. For example, tools like 'Metasploit' are continually updated to include new exploits and payloads.

Background: The Genesis of Kali Linux

To appreciate the power and potential of Kali Linux fully, we must delve into its roots. Kali Linux emerged from the fusion of 'BackTrack,' its predecessor, and the visionary thinking of Offensive Security.

The Legacy of BackTrack

BackTrack, a forerunner in the world of security-focused Linux distributions, was celebrated for its extensive collection of hacking tools. Security professionals favored it, and it became synonymous with ethical hacking and penetration testing. For example, it included 'Aircrack-ng,' a tool used for testing the security of wireless networks.

However, BackTrack wasn't without its limitations. As technology advanced, so did the challenges. The need for a more refined and dynamic platform became evident. The development team recognized these evolving demands and set out to create a platform that would not just meet but surpass these expectations.

The Birth of Kali Linux

In 2013, Kali Linux was born, a purposeful creation designed to cater to the specific needs of ethical hackers, security enthusiasts, and penetration testers. It emerged from a commitment to excellence in cybersecurity.

Kali Linux adopted a Debian base, providing a solid foundation. The transition from BackTrack to Kali Linux was more than just a change of name; it was a commitment to providing a more robust and user-friendly platform. Offensive Security, a prominent organization in the cybersecurity training and certification field, spearheaded this venture.

The Ethical Hacking Philosophy

Kali Linux isn't just a collection of tools; it embodies a philosophy that emphasizes the responsible and lawful use of hacking skills. Ethical hacking is about using these skills for the greater good, to uncover vulnerabilities, and secure digital assets. The platform serves as a haven for hands-on learning and growth in the realm of cybersecurity.

GETTING STARTED WITH KALI LINUX

Now that we understand the background and potential of Kali Linux, let's take our first steps into this powerful world. We'll start by installing and setting up Kali Linux, ensuring that you're ready to harness its full potential.

Step 1: Download Kali Linux

Begin by visiting the official Kali Linux website (https://www.kali.org) and navigate to the "Downloads" section. Here, you'll find various installation images for different platforms. Select the one that suits your system architecture, such as 64-bit or 32-bit.

Step 2: Create a Bootable USB Drive (Optional)

If you're installing Kali Linux on a physical machine, you can create a bootable USB drive using software like Rufus (for

Windows) or balenaEtcher (cross-platform). This step is optional if you're setting up Kali Linux in a virtual machine.

Step 3: Install Kali Linux

Boot your computer from the Kali Linux installation media (USB drive or ISO file). Follow the on-screen prompts to select your language, location, and keyboard layout. When prompted to configure the network, ensure you have internet access as Kali Linux may need to download additional packages during installation.

Step 4: Set Up User Accounts

During installation, you'll be prompted to set a root password (the superuser) and create a standard user account. Make sure to choose strong and unique passwords.

Step 5: Choose a Desktop Environment (Optional)

Kali Linux offers different desktop environments, including Xfce, GNOME, and KDE. Choose the one that suits your preferences. Xfce, for example, offers a lightweight and fast desktop environment, while GNOME provides a more modern and feature-rich experience.

Step 6: Install Kali Linux

Once you've configured your user accounts and chosen your desktop environment, the installation process will begin. This may take some time, as it involves copying the necessary files to your system.

Step 7: Update Kali Linux

After the installation is complete, it's essential to keep Kali Linux up to date.

```
1    sudo apt update sudo apt upgrade
```

This ensures that you have the latest security updates and software patches.

Step 8: Customize Your Environment

Now that you have Kali Linux up and running, you can customize your environment to suit your needs. This includes installing additional tools, adjusting system settings, and configuring your desktop environment.

For instance, you can install tools like 'Burp Suite' for web application testing or 'Hashcat' for password cracking. To install a tool, use the following command, replacing **<tool_name>** with the name of the tool:

```
1    sudo apt install <tool_name>
```

You can also explore Kali Linux's control panel, where you can configure various system settings and personalize your desktop environment.

Exploring Kali Linux's Tools

Kali Linux's true power lies in its extensive toolkit. Let's take a closer look at some of the tools you'll find within Kali Linux:

1. Nmap (Network Mapper)

Nmap is a versatile network scanning tool used to discover devices, open ports, and services running on a network. For example, to scan a local network for active hosts, use the following command:

```
1    nmap -sn 192.168.1.0/24
```

This command will scan all IP addresses from 192.168.1.1 to 192.168.1.254 to identify active hosts.

2. Wireshark

Wireshark is a powerful packet analyzer that allows you to capture and inspect data on a network. For example, you can use Wireshark to analyze network traffic to and from a specific device, helping identify potential security issues.

3. Metasploit Framework

Metasploit is a penetration testing framework used for exploiting vulnerabilities in systems. It's an essential tool for ethical hackers. For example, you can use Metasploit to test a system's susceptibility to specific exploits or vulnerabilities.

4. Aircrack-ng

Aircrack-ng is a set of tools used for testing and securing wireless networks. For example, you can use Aircrack-ng to capture and crack WPA/WPA2 passwords, helping to secure your own network against potential attacks.

5. Foremost

Foremost is a digital forensics tool used to recover lost files from storage devices. For example, if you're investigating a compromised system, you can use Foremost to recover deleted files and uncover evidence.

The platform provides tools for various purposes, from information gathering to vulnerability assessment and digital forensics.

Unleash Your Full Potential

In this section, you've gained a foundational understanding of Kali Linux, its significance in the world of ethical hacking, and the tools it provides. We've taken our first steps in setting up Kali Linux, and you've been introduced to some of the essential tools within its vast arsenal.

With Kali Linux at your disposal, you're ready to embark on a journey into the world of ethical hacking and cybersecurity. As you continue your exploration, remember that knowledge and tools are your greatest assets. In the upcoming sections, we'll dive deeper into specific aspects of Kali Linux, honing your skills and knowledge to unlock its full potential.

Are you ready to unleash the power of Kali Linux and become a digital warrior in the realm of ethical hacking? Join us as we delve deeper into this exciting journey, where the cybersecurity landscape unfolds before you, full of challenges and opportunities.

The Genesis of Kali Linux

To understand the full potential of Kali Linux, we must first explore its origins and the philosophy that drives its evolution. Born from the fusion of BackTrack and developed by Offensive Security, Kali Linux emerged as a response to the growing demand for a sophisticated and user-friendly penetration testing platform.

BackTrack, the predecessor of Kali Linux, was celebrated for its comprehensive set of hacking tools, making it a favorite among security professionals. However, it was not without its limitations. As technology advanced, so did the need for a more refined and dynamic toolset. Thus, Kali Linux was born in 2013, designed to surpass its predecessor in both functionality and usability.

The Essence of Kali Linux

At its core, Kali Linux is more than just an operating system; it's a commitment to excellence in cybersecurity. It encapsulates the very essence of ethical hacking, offering an extensive toolkit that empowers you to test and strengthen the security of networks, systems, and applications. This chapter will guide you through the heart of Kali Linux, providing you with the foundational knowledge needed to wield this powerful instrument effectively.

Navigating Kali Linux

Kali Linux is renowned not only for its technical capabilities but also for its accessibility. Whether you are a seasoned cybersecurity professional or a newcomer to the field, Kali Linux ensures a smooth journey into the world of ethical hacking. It provides a user-friendly interface, offering a balance between simplicity and functionality.

The Kali Linux Toolkit

One of the most prominent features of Kali Linux is its toolkit, which houses a staggering array of over 600 pre-installed tools, each tailored to meet the specific needs of ethical hackers, penetration testers, and security enthusiasts. This vast arsenal includes tools for information gathering, vulnerability assessment, network scanning, wireless attacks, and digital forensics, among others. With Kali Linux, you have the right tool for every security challenge at your fingertips.

The Art of Ethical Hacking

Kali Linux goes beyond being a mere toolbox; it is a gateway to the art of ethical hacking. It provides an environment where you can apply your knowledge, explore vulnerabilities, and gain hands-on experience in a safe and controlled setting. It is not just about using tools but developing a profound understanding of the cybersecurity landscape, uncovering vulnerabilities, and learning how to mitigate them.

Keeping Up with the Times

In the ever-changing world of cybersecurity, staying current is of utmost importance. Kali Linux is committed to continuous improvement. The Kali Linux team maintains a strict update schedule, ensuring that tools are always up to date. This dedication guarantees that you're working with the latest and most effective tools available, which is essential in a field that evolves rapidly.

ADVANCED CUSTOMIZATION AND CONFIGURATION

In the previous section, we explored the fundamentals of setting up Kali Linux, delving into its background and the powerful tools it offers. Now, it's time to take our journey a step further. Advanced customization and configuration of Kali Linux will allow you to tailor the operating system to your specific needs, enhancing your efficiency and effectiveness as an ethical hacker or security professional.

Tailoring Your Kali Linux Environment

Kali Linux, in its default configuration, is a versatile and powerful platform. However, to truly unleash its potential, you should consider fine-tuning and personalizing it to match your workflow and preferences. Let's delve into some advanced customization options that will empower you to do just that.

1. Personalizing the Desktop Environment

Kali Linux offers multiple desktop environments, including Xfce, GNOME, and KDE. Each has its unique look, feel, and features. By selecting the one that resonates with you, you can enhance your user experience. Here's how to change your desktop environment:

- **Xfce**: A lightweight and efficient option that conserves system resources. It is a great choice for older hardware or users who prefer a simple and snappy interface.

To install Xfce:

```
1    sudo apt install kali-desktop-xfce
```

- **GNOME**: A popular and modern desktop environment known for its user-friendly interface and customization options.

To install GNOME:

```
1    sudo apt install kali-desktop-gnome
```

- **KDE**: A visually appealing and feature-rich desktop environment that provides a highly customizable experience.

To install KDE:

```
1    sudo apt install kali-desktop-kde
```

After installation, you can select your preferred desktop environment from the login screen.

2. Adding and Removing Software

Kali Linux provides a broad selection of pre-installed tools, but your specific tasks may require additional software. You can customize your software arsenal by installing or removing packages as needed.

- **To install software**, you can use the **apt** package manager. For instance, if you want to install the 'Sublime Text' text editor, you can use the following command:

```
1    sudo apt install sublime-text
```

- **To remove software**, you can use the same **apt** package manager. To remove 'Sublime Text', you would use:

```
1    sudo apt remove sublime-text
```

3. Tweaking the Terminal

The terminal is your primary interface for interacting with Kali Linux. Customizing it can significantly improve your workflow. Here are a few tips:

- **Change the terminal emulator**: Kali Linux comes with the default terminal emulator 'GNOME Terminal.' You can install alternatives like 'Konsole' or 'Terminator' for different features and aesthetics.

To install Konsole:

```
1    sudo apt install konsole
```

- **Customize the terminal appearance**: You can adjust the terminal's font, colors, and transparency to make it visually pleasing and easy to use. Explore the terminal's preferences to find options for customization.

4. Shell Configuration

Kali Linux typically uses the Bash shell (Bourne-Again Shell) as its default command-line interpreter. The shell configuration files, such as **.bashrc**, allow you to customize your shell environment.

- **Aliases**: Create aliases for commonly used commands to save time and reduce typing. For example, you can create an alias to update your system with a single command:

```
1    alias update='sudo apt update && sudo apt upgrade'
```

- **Environment Variables**: You can set environment variables to influence how your shell behaves. For instance, you can set the **PS1** variable to change your command prompt's appearance.

To change the command prompt to display the current directory:

```
1    export PS1="\w $ "
```

5. Expanding Your Toolkit

Kali Linux's vast collection of pre-installed tools is impressive, but there are always specialized tools that may be beneficial for your specific tasks. You can expand your toolkit by installing additional tools and scripts.

For example, if you are involved in wireless security assessments, you might want to install 'Airodump-ng' for capturing wireless packets:

```
1    sudo apt install aircrack-ng
```

6. Custom Scripting and Automation

Scripting and automation can significantly enhance your efficiency. You can create custom scripts to automate repetitive tasks or perform specific functions. Python and Bash are popular scripting languages used by many Kali Linux users.

As an example, let's say you often need to scan your local network using Nmap.

```
1    #!/bin/bash nmap -sn 192.168.1.0/24
```

After creating the script and making it executable with **chmod +x scriptname.sh**, you can run it with a single command.

7. System Hardening

While Kali Linux is designed for security testing, it's essential to maintain the security of the system itself. Consider implementing measures to harden your Kali Linux installation, such as:

- The 'ufw' (Uncomplicated Firewall) is a user-friendly option.

To install ufw:

```
1    sudo apt install ufw
```

- **Regular Updates**: Keep your system up to date with the latest security patches.

```
1    sudo apt update sudo apt upgrade
```

- **Root Access**: Minimize the use of the root account, as working as a regular user and using **sudo** when necessary reduces the risk of accidental system changes.

These advanced customization and configuration options empower you to tailor Kali Linux to your specific needs. By personalizing your environment, expanding your toolkit, and optimizing your workflow, you can make the most of this powerful platform and become a more effective ethical hacker or security professional.

Are you ready to take the next step in fine-tuning your Kali Linux installation to match your unique requirements and enhance your productivity? Let's explore advanced customization and configuration further, allowing you to unlock the full potential of this versatile operating system.

CHAPTER 2: THE ART OF RECONNAISSANCE

Welcome to Chapter 2 of our journey into the realm of ethical hacking with Kali Linux. In the previous chapter, we laid the foundation by exploring the genesis of Kali Linux, understanding its essence, and setting up the environment. Now, it's time to dive deeper into the art of ethical hacking.

In this chapter, we'll focus on advanced information gathering techniques, going beyond the basics and equipping you with the skills and knowledge needed to become a proficient digital detective. Information gathering is the first and critical phase in any hacking endeavor. It provides the reconnaissance and intelligence needed to plan and execute successful attacks, as well as to strengthen the security of your own systems.

The Importance of Information Gathering

Before we delve into advanced techniques, let's reiterate why information gathering is indispensable in the world of cybersecurity and ethical hacking.

1. Target Identification

```
1   Information gathering helps you identify your target,
2   whether it's a website, a network, or an individual system. Knowing your target is the first step
3   in any successful hacking operation.
```

2. Vulnerability Assessment

```
1   Information gathering uncovers vulnerabilities
2   and weaknesses in the target system.
3   This phase is vital for ethical hackers
4   because it allows them to alert organizations
5   or system owners to security gaps before malicious hackers exploit them.
```

3. Attack Surface Mapping

```
1   An attack surface includes all the entry points
2   and potential vulnerabilities in a system or network.
3   Information gathering provides insights into this surface,
4   enabling ethical hackers to explore and exploit it effectively.
```

4. Social Engineering

```
1   Information gathering goes beyond technical aspects
2   and extends to social engineering.
3   It helps gather information about people, their habits,
4   and their vulnerabilities,
5   which can be exploited through various means.
```

5. Stealth and Evasion

```
1   A good ethical hacker is stealthy,
2   evading detection while conducting reconnaissance.
3   Information gathering techniques
4   play a crucial role in remaining hidden from the target system.
5   Now that we understand the significance of information gathering
6   let's explore advanced techniques and tools
7   that will enable you to collect valuable data effectively.
```

Leveraging Advanced Information Gathering Techniques

1. OSINT (Open-Source Intelligence)

```
1   OSINT is a goldmine of information gathered from publicly available sources such as social media,
2   news articles, government records, and more. Ethical hackers can harness OSINT to collect data about their targets.
3   Tools like 'theHarvester' can help automate this process,
4   gathering information about email addresses,
5   subdomains, and more. - **theHarvester Usage**: ``` bash theharvester -d example.com -l 500 -b google
6   ``` This command uses 'theHarvester'
7   to gather information about the domain 'example.com' from Google, returning up to 500 results.
```

2. DNS Enumeration and Subdomain Discovery

```
1   DNS (Domain Name System) enumeration and subdomain discovery are essential
2   for mapping the target's attack surface.
3   Tools like 'dnsenum' and 'Sublist3r' assist in this process.
4   They query DNS servers to reveal information about domain names and subdomains. -
5   **dnsenum Usage**: ``` bash dnsenum example.com ``` Running 'dnsenum' against
6   'example.com' provides information about the DNS configuration of the domain.
7   - **Sublist3r Usage**:
8   ``` bash python sublist3r.py -d example.com ```
9   'Sublist3r' is used to discover subdomains associated with 'example.com.'
```

3. Port Scanning

```
1   Port scanning is a crucial technique to identify open ports on target systems.
2   'Nmap' is a versatile and widely used tool for port scanning.
3   By identifying open ports, you can pinpoint potential entry points into the system.
4   - **Nmap Usage**: ``` bash nmap -p- -T4 example.com ```
5   This command scans all ports of 'example.com'
6   and provides information about open ports and their associated services.
```

4. Vulnerability Scanning

```
1   Vulnerability scanning tools like 'Nessus' and 'OpenVAS'
2   allow you to identify security weaknesses within the target system.
3   These tools perform extensive scans
4   and provide reports on potential vulnerabilities. -
5   **Nessus Usage**: After installing Nessus and setting up the scanner,
6   access it through a web browser and create a new scan policy.
7   Then, initiate a scan against the target system to identify vulnerabilities. -
8   **OpenVAS Usage**:
9   OpenVAS operates similarly to Nessus and offers
10  a web-based interface for creating and launching scans.
```

5. Active Reconnaissance

```
1   Active reconnaissance techniques involve interacting
2   directly with the target system to gather information.
3   Tools like 'Maltego' and 'Shodan' provide actionable data by querying the target or related systems. -
4   **Maltego Usage**: Maltego is a powerful information gathering tool.
5   After configuring it with your API key,
6   you can perform extensive searches and data correlation to
7   build comprehensive profiles of your target. -
8   **Shodan Usage**: Shodan is known as the search engine for IoT devices.
9   By using specific search queries,
10  you can discover vulnerable devices on the internet.
11  For example, you can search for webcams using the query 'webcam.'
```

6. Social Engineering and Phishing

```
1   Information gathering isn't limited to technical aspects.
2   Social engineering and phishing techniques rely on human psychology and behavior.
3   Tools like 'Social-Engineer Toolkit (SET)' aid in crafting and launching social engineering attacks. -
4   **SET Usage**: The Social-Engineer Toolkit simplifies the process of creating phishing attacks.
5   You can use it to craft convincing email
6   or website-based attacks and launch them against your target.
```

7. Exploiting Online Databases

```
1   Many websites and organizations inadvertently expose sensitive information through
2   insecure databases.
3   Tools like 'sqlmap' are designed to identify and exploit such vulnerabilities. -
4   **sqlmap Usage**:
5   Sqlmap is used to detect and exploit SQL injection vulnerabilities.
6   To test a website for SQL injection, you can use a command like:
7   ```bash sqlmap -u "http://example.com/page?id=1" --dbs ```
8   This command checks the URL 'http://example.com/page?id=1'
9   for potential SQL injection vulnerabilities.
```

8. In-Depth Reconnaissance with Metasploit

```
1   Metasploit isn't just a penetration testing tool;
2   it's also a valuable source of information about vulnerabilities.
3   You can use Metasploit to search for known vulnerabilities in target systems. -
4   **Metasploit Usage**:
5   Launch Metasploit and use the search command to look for specific vulnerabilities or exploits.
6   For example, you can search for 'WordPress' vulnerabilities: ```bash search WordPress ```
7   This command returns a list of available modules related to 'WordPress' vulnerabilities.
```

9. Intelligence Gathering with IntelligenceX

```
{} IntelligenceX is a search engine for fin Untitled 1 2  ●
1    IntelligenceX is a search engine for finding intelligence and corporate data on the internet.
2    It allows you to search for keywords, domains, and email addresses to gather information about a target.
3    _ **IntelligenceX Usage**: Visit the IntelligenceX website (https://intelx.io/)
4    and enter the search query related to your target.
5    The search results will provide valuable information.
```

TARGET PROFILING AND FOOTPRINTING

In the vast landscape of ethical hacking and cybersecurity, the process of information gathering extends far beyond basic reconnaissance. To become a proficient digital detective, you must delve into advanced techniques that encompass every aspect of your target. Target profiling and footprinting, the focus of this section, are fundamental components of this process, allowing you to create a comprehensive profile of your target, be it an individual, an organization, or a network.

The Significance of Target Profiling

Before we delve into the intricacies of target profiling, let's reaffirm why it holds a pivotal role in ethical hacking:

1. Understanding the Target's Behavior

SQL

```
1   Target profiling delves into understanding the behavior,
2   habits, and patterns of your target.
3   This information can be invaluable
4   when crafting social engineering attacks or predicting user actions.
```

2. Attack Surface Mapping

Vbnet

```
1   An ethical hacker's mission is to identify
2   and exploit vulnerabilities in the target system.
3   Profiling helps in mapping the attack surface,
4   determining entry points, and discovering weak links.
```

3. Tailoring Attacks

Vbnet

```
1   Profiling enables you to customize your attacks for maximum effectiveness.
2   By understanding the target's preferences and weaknesses,
3   you can craft more convincing phishing emails or design attacks that align with their interests.
```

4. Security Strengthening

Vbnet

```
1   On the flip side, profiling can serve as a security-enhancement tool.
2   Organizations can use the same techniques to identify potential vulnerabilities
3   and weak spots in their systems or personnel.
```

With these points in mind, let's explore advanced techniques for target profiling and footprinting.

Leveraging Advanced Target Profiling Techniques

1. Social Media Analysis

Vbnet

```
1   Social media platforms are treasure troves of personal information.
2   Ethical hackers can gather data from platforms like Facebook,
3   LinkedIn, Twitter, and Instagram to build detailed profiles.
4   Tools like 'SpiderFoot' automate this process by scraping public data.
5   - **SpiderFoot Usage**: SpiderFoot is an open-source reconnaissance tool.
6   To use it, you need to install and configure it.
7   Then, run the following command to perform a scan:
8   ```bash python3 sf.py -d target.com ``` This command initiates a scan of the domain
9   'target.com' to gather information from various sources.
```

2. Domain Profiling

Less

```
1   Profiling a target's domain is essential, especially when conducting external assessments.
2   Tools like 'Whois' and 'DomainTools' provide details about domain ownership, registration, and history.
3   - **Whois Usage**: To retrieve WHOIS information for a domain, use a command like: ```bash whois target.com ```
4   This command returns detailed registration information for the domain 'target.com.'
```

3. Email Harvesting and Analysis

SQL

```
1   Email addresses are key to social engineering attacks and targeted phishing.
2   Tools like 'theHarvester' and 'HarvestMail' help collect and analyze email addresses associated with a target.
3   **theHarvester Usage**: As mentioned earlier,
4   you can use 'theHarvester' to collect email addresses associated with a domain.
5   For example: ```bash theharvester -d target.com -l 500 -b google ```
6   This command gathers email addresses associated with the domain 'target.com' from Google search results.
```

4. IP Geolocation and Tracing

Perl

```
Understanding the physical location of a Untitled-1 ●
1    Understanding the physical location of a target can be advantageous.
2    Tools like 'IPinfo' and 'Traceroute' help you trace the geographic location of an IP address.
3    - **IPinfo Usage**: To geolocate an IP address, you can use the 'ipinfo'
4    command followed by the IP address you want to trace: ```bash ipinfo 8.8.8.8 ```
5    This command provides information about the geographical location of the IP address.
```

5. Network Enumeration

Vbnet

```
1    When targeting an organization or network,
2    enumerating network resources and services is essential.
3    Tools like 'NetDiscover' and 'nmap' can assist in this process.
4    - **NetDiscover Usage**:
5    NetDiscover is a network scanning tool.
6    To discover devices on your local network, you can use a command like:
7    ```bash sudo netdiscover -r 192.168.1.0/24 ```
8    This command scans the IP range '192.168.1.0/24' for active devices.
```

6. Website Analysis and Profiling

Python

```
1    When dealing with web applications or websites,
2    it's crucial to analyze and profile them for vulnerabilities and weaknesses.
3    Tools like 'Wappalyzer' and 'BuiltWith' can reveal the technologies
4    and frameworks used by the target site.
5    - **Wappalyzer Usage**:
6    Wappalyzer is a browser extension that provides insights into the technologies used by a website.
7    Install the extension in your browser,
8    and it will automatically detect and display the technologies used by the sites you visit.
```

7. Document Metadata Extraction

Vbnet

```
1    Documents often contain hidden metadata,
2    which can disclose information about the document's author, revisions, and editing history.
3    Tools like 'ExifTool' and 'mat2' help extract metadata from files.
4    - **ExifTool Usage**: ExifTool is a versatile tool for extracting metadata from various file types.
5    To extract metadata from a document, use a command like:
6    ```bash exiftool document.docx ```
7    This command provides detailed metadata about the document.
```

Conclusion

Target profiling and footprinting are essential components of advanced information gathering techniques in ethical hacking. By utilizing these tools and methods, you can build comprehensive profiles of your targets, enhance the precision of your attacks, and identify potential vulnerabilities that require attention. Whether you are an ethical hacker seeking to strengthen security or an attacker exploring weaknesses, these techniques are your guide to understanding your digital terrain.

As you continue your journey into the realm of ethical hacking, remember that knowledge and responsible use of these techniques are your greatest assets. The upcoming sections will further refine your skills and provide you with tools and knowledge to become a proficient digital detective in the ever-evolving world of cybersecurity.

CHAPTER 3: VULNERABILITY ASSESSMENT

SCANNING AND IDENTIFYING SYSTEM WEAKNESSES

Welcome to Chapter 3 of our exploration into the world of ethical hacking with Kali Linux. In the previous chapters, we laid the foundation by understanding the essence of Kali Linux and mastering advanced information gathering techniques. As we move forward, we venture into the critical domain of vulnerability assessment.

Vulnerability assessment is a pivotal phase in ethical hacking, acting as the bridge between information gathering and penetration testing. In this chapter, we will delve into the art of scanning and identifying system weaknesses, equipping you with the skills to identify and address vulnerabilities in target systems. This process is essential for both ethical hackers looking to strengthen security and those aiming to exploit weaknesses.

The Role of Vulnerability Assessment

Before we embark on the journey of vulnerability assessment, it's crucial to grasp the significance of this phase in the realm of ethical hacking:

1. System Hardening

Vbnet

```
1   Vulnerability assessment is an essential tool for organizations to identify and mitigate weaknesses within their systems.
2   By detecting vulnerabilities, they can take proactive measures to enhance security.
```

2. Ethical Hacking

Vbnet Copy code

```
1   For ethical hackers,
2   vulnerability assessment is the first step towards
3   identifying potential entry points for exploitation.
4   It's a systematic approach to recognizing and understanding system weaknesses.
```

3. Security Compliance

CSS Copy code

```
1   Many industries and organizations have specific security standards and compliance requirements.
2   Vulnerability assessment is a means of ensuring that systems adhere to these standards.
```

4. Risk Mitigation

VBNET Copy code

```
1    Understanding vulnerabilities is crucial for assessing risks.
2    By identifying potential threats,
3    organizations can prioritize and implement risk mitigation measu
```

With these points in mind, we'll explore advanced techniques for scanning and identifying system weaknesses.

MASTERING VULNERABILITY ASSESSMENT TECHNIQUES

1. Network Scanning with Nmap

PERL COPY CODE

```
Nmap, a powerful open-source tool, is a staple in the arsenal of ethical hackers.
It excels in network scanning and identifying open ports, services, and potential vulnerabilities.
- **Nmap Usage**:
To scan a target system and identify open ports, you can use the following command:
```bash nmap -T4 -p- target.com ```
This command conducts a thorough scan of 'target.com,'
discovering open ports and the services running on them.
```

2. Detecting Web Application Vulnerabilities with Nikto

Less Copy code

```
Nikto is a web application scanner that specializes in identifying potential
vulnerabilities and weaknesses in web servers
and applications.
It provides a comprehensive assessment of a web application's security.
- **Nikto Usage**: To scan a web application, use the following command:
```bash nikto -h https://webapp.com ```
This command scans the web application at 'https://webapp.com' for vulnerabilities.
```

3. Database Scanning with SQLMap

Vbnet Copy code

```
SQL injection is a common vulnerability in web applications.
SQLMap is a specialized tool for detecting and exploiting these vulnerabilities,
allowing you to access and manipulate databases. - **SQLMap Usage**:
To test a web application for SQL injection, you can use a command like:
  ```bash sqlmap -u "https://webapp.com/login.php"
  --data="username=test&password=test" --cookie="PHPSESSID=test" --level=5 --risk=3 --dbs
  ``` This command tests 'https://webapp.com/login.php' for SQL injection and identifies the databases present.
```

4. Service Enumeration with Enum4linux

Vbnet Copy code

```
Enum4linux is a tool designed for identifying
and extracting information from Windows machines and domains.
It's a valuable asset for enumerating Windows systems.
  - **Enum4linux Usage**: To enumerate a Windows machine,
use a command like:
```bash enum4linux -A target_ip ```
This command provides detailed information about the target Windows machine.
```

5. Vulnerability Scanning with Nessus

Less Copy code

```
Nessus is a widely used vulnerability scanner that can identify
and report vulnerabilities in target systems.
It offers a user-friendly interface and extensive database of known vulnerabilities.
  - **Nessus Usage**: After configuring Nessus,
you can create a new scan policy
and launch a scan against the target system to identify vulnerabilities.
```

6. Wireless Network Assessment with Airodump-ng

Kotlin Copy code

```
Airodump-ng is a part of the Aircrack-ng suite and is used for wireless network assessments.
It can discover wireless networks, capture data, and identify potential vulnerabilities.
  - **Airodump-ng Usage**:
To discover and capture data from nearby wireless networks, use a command like:
```bash airodump-ng wlan0 ```
This command lists nearby wireless networks and captures data packets.
```

Vulnerability assessment is the backbone of ethical hacking and cybersecurity. By mastering the techniques and tools presented in this chapter, you can become a proficient digital detective, capable of scanning and identifying weaknesses in target systems. Whether your goal is to strengthen security or exploit vulnerabilities responsibly, these skills are essential in the ever-evolving landscape of cybersecurity.

As we progress through this journey, you will gain a deeper understanding of ethical hacking and cybersecurity. In the following sections, we will further refine your skills and knowledge, equipping you with the expertise to excel in this dynamic field.

EXPLOITING NETWORK SERVICES

Now that we've covered scanning and identifying system weaknesses, it's time to explore the next step: exploiting network services. Understanding vulnerabilities and open ports is only part of the equation. Ethical hackers must also be proficient in exploiting these weaknesses to assess the impact and potential risks.

Step-by-Step Guide:

1. **Identify Vulnerable Services**: Begin by using scanning tools like Nmap to identify open ports and

vulnerable services on the target system. These services are often associated with specific vulnerabilities that can be exploited.

2. **Research Vulnerabilities**: Once you've identified the services, research the vulnerabilities associated with them. Resources like the Common Vulnerabilities and Exposures (CVE) database and vendor advisories can provide detailed information.

3. **Select Appropriate Exploits**: Find or develop exploits that target the identified vulnerabilities. This step may involve searching for existing exploit code, crafting your own, or modifying existing exploits to suit the target.

4. **Configure the Exploits**: Ensure that the chosen exploits are properly configured for the target system. This may involve specifying the target's IP address, port, and other relevant parameters.

5. **Run the Exploits**: Execute the exploits to test whether the identified vulnerabilities can be successfully exploited. Pay close attention to the results and any error messages to fine-tune the process.

6. **Analyze the Impact**: After a successful exploit, assess the impact on the target system. Understand what level of access or control you've gained and what actions can be performed.

7. **Document Findings**: Comprehensive documentation is crucial. Record the details of the exploit, including the vulnerability, the exploit used, and the impact on the target system.

8. **Recommend Mitigation**: As an ethical hacker, it's important to provide recommendations for mitigating the identified vulnerabilities. Offer solutions or strategies to improve security.

Post-Exploitation Techniques

The process of ethical hacking doesn't stop at gaining initial access to a target system. Post-exploitation is an integral part of the assessment, where ethical hackers aim to maintain access, gather more information, and achieve specific goals within the compromised system.

Step-by-Step Guide:

1. **Maintain Access**: Ensure continued access to the compromised system. This may involve creating

backdoors, establishing persistence mechanisms, or maintaining a foothold through various means.

2. **Privilege Escalation**: Seek ways to escalate privileges within the compromised system. Exploiting vulnerabilities or misconfigurations can grant higher levels of access and control.

3. **Lateral Movement**: Move laterally within the target network to explore and compromise other systems. Use techniques like pass-the-hash, token impersonation, or remote code execution to extend your reach.

4. **Data Collection**: Gather valuable information from the compromised system. This may include sensitive files, user credentials, configurations, and any data relevant to the assessment's objectives.

5. **Cover Tracks**: Ensure that your activities within the compromised system remain discreet. Delete logs, clear event records, and cover your tracks to avoid detection.

6. **Achieve Objectives**: If your ethical hacking engagement has specific objectives, work toward accomplishing them. This could involve accessing a

particular system, stealing sensitive data, or demonstrating specific vulnerabilities.

7. **Exit Strategy**: Plan your exit strategy carefully. Ensure that you leave the compromised system in a secure state and without any lasting damage. Document the actions you've taken.

8. **Final Reporting**: As with all phases of ethical hacking, comprehensive reporting is crucial. Document the post-exploitation activities, the data collected, and any actions taken within the compromised system.

In this chapter, we've explored exploiting network services and post-exploitation techniques, which are essential components of an ethical hacking engagement. As we continue our journey, you'll further refine your skills and knowledge, gaining expertise in various aspects of cybersecurity and ethical hacking.

Navigating the Landscape of Exploitable Targets

As we delve deeper into the realm of ethical hacking, it becomes imperative to understand the intricacies of navigating the landscape of exploitable targets. This section will serve as your guide to identifying, selecting, and prioritizing potential targets for your ethical hacking endeavors. Ethical hackers are not aimlessly scanning the vast digital terrain for vulnerabilities; they follow a structured approach that maximizes their effectiveness while minimizing risks.

THE IMPORTANCE OF TARGET SELECTION

Selecting the right target is the cornerstone of ethical hacking. This decision is not arbitrary; it's a strategic choice that hinges on several crucial factors. A thoughtful selection process enhances the efficiency and success of your ethical hacking engagement. Let's explore why target selection is so vital:

1. Focused Effort

Css Copy code

```
Choosing the right target allows you to channel your efforts effectively.
Instead of dispersing your resources,
you concentrate on a specific area or system, optimizing your chances of success.
```

2. Legal and Ethical Compliance

Vbnet Copy code

```
Ethical hackers must always operate within the bounds of the law and ethical guidelines.
Target selection is a key aspect of ensuring that you are not
infringing on the rights or privacy of unintended entities.
```

3. Risk Mitigation

Csharp Copy code

```
A well-chosen target minimizes the potential risks associated with ethical hacking.
It prevents accidental damage or data breaches that could harm innocent parties.
```

4. Objective Achievement

Css Copy code

```
Ethical hacking engagements often have predefined objectives.
The right target aligns with these objectives,
allowing you to fulfill your mission
and provide valuable insights to clients or organizations.
```

5. Resource Optimization

Sql Copy code

```
Resources, including time and expertise, are finite.
Selecting the right target ensures that these resources are used efficiently,
providing the best return on investment.
```

With these considerations in mind, let's embark on a step-by-step guide to navigating the landscape of exploitable targets.

Step 1: Define Objectives

The first step in selecting an exploitable target is to define your objectives clearly. Your objectives should encompass what you aim to achieve through your ethical hacking engagement. These objectives may include:

- **Strengthening Security**: Identifying vulnerabilities in a target system to help the organization improve its security.

- **Data Protection**: Ensuring the security of sensitive data, such as customer information or intellectual property.

- **Compliance Testing**: Ensuring that a system or network adheres to regulatory standards and compliance requirements.

- **Security Awareness**: Demonstrating the potential risks to an organization to raise security awareness.

- **Penetration Testing**: Simulating cyberattacks to test the effectiveness of security measures.

The objectives you define will shape your target selection process, guiding you toward systems and areas that align with your goals.

Step 2: Identify Potential Targets

Once you have a clear set of objectives, the next step is to identify potential targets. These can be systems, networks, web applications, or any digital entity that falls within the scope of your objectives.

1. Scope Agreement

Sql Copy code

```
Ensure that your potential targets fall
within the agreed-upon scope of your ethical hacking engagement.
This is crucial for legal and ethical compliance.
```

2. Critical Assets

Sql Copy code

```
Identify critical assets within the organization or system.
These assets are typically high-value and may include customer databases,
financial systems, or intellectual property.
```

3. Known Vulnerabilities

Python Copy code

```
Prioritize targets that are known to have vulnerabilities.
Publicly available information,
such as vulnerability databases, can help identify systems with documented weaknesses.
```

4. System Dependencies

Vbnet Copy code

```
A system that is critical to an organization's operations may be a more attractive target.
consider the dependencies of the potential targets.
```

Step 3: Assess Legal and Ethical Considerations

Before finalizing your target selection, it's imperative to assess legal and ethical considerations. Ethical hackers must operate within the boundaries of the law and adhere to ethical guidelines. Consider the following legal and ethical factors:

1. Permission and Authorization

Vbnet Copy code

```
Ensure that you have proper permission
and authorization to conduct ethical hacking activities on the chosen target.
Unauthorized hacking can lead to legal repercussions.
```

2. Data Privacy

Sql Copy code

```
Respect data privacy laws and regulations,
particularly when dealing with systems that store sensitive information.
```

3. Non-Disclosure Agreements (NDAs)

Csharp Copy code

```
If you are bound by an NDA or other contractual agreements,
ensure that your target selection complies with these agreements.
```

4. Innocent Parties

Css Copy code

```
Verify that the target selection does not involve innocent parties
or entities unrelated to the objectives of your ethical hacking engagement.
```

Step 4: Risk Assessment

After identifying potential targets and assessing legal and ethical considerations, conduct a risk assessment. Evaluate the potential risks associated with each target, considering the following factors:

1. Impact of a Breach

Csharp Copy code

```
Assess the impact of a security breach on the target.
What are the consequences if a vulnerability is exploited?
```

2. Likelihood of Detection

Vbnet Copy code

```
Consider the likelihood of your ethical hacking activities being detected
by security measures or the target's administrators.
```

3. Recovery Capabilities

Vbnet Copy code

```
Evaluate the target's ability to recover from a security incident.
Some systems may have robust recovery measures in place.
```

4. Cascading Effects

Css Copy code

```
Analyze whether a breach in the target system
could lead to cascading effects that impact other systems or entities.
```

Step 5: Prioritize Targets

Based on your risk assessment, prioritize the potential targets. Prioritization ensures that you focus your efforts on the most critical and valuable targets. Consider the following prioritization criteria:

1. Criticality

Csharp Copy code

```
Targets that, if compromised,
could result in severe consequences should be high on your priority list.
```

2. Likelihood of Success

Sql Copy code

```
Prioritize targets with a higher likelihood of success.
These are typically systems with known vulnerabilities or weaknesses.
```

3. Relevance to Objectives

Perl Copy code

```
Targets that directly align with your defined objectives should be given higher priority.
```

4. Ethical and Legal Implications

Css Copy code

```
Targets that have fewer ethical and legal implications
should be prioritized to mitigate potential risks.
```

Step 6: Finalize the Selection

With your objectives, potential targets, legal and ethical considerations, risk assessment, and prioritization in mind, finalize your selection. The selected target should be the one that best aligns with your goals and minimizes potential risks.

Conclusion

Navigating the landscape of exploitable targets is a fundamental aspect of ethical hacking. It requires a structured and strategic approach that takes into account objectives, legal and ethical considerations, risk assessment, and prioritization. By following these steps, ethical hackers ensure that their efforts are focused, efficient, and aligned with the desired outcomes of their engagements. Target selection is not only about finding vulnerabilities; it's about making responsible and ethical choices in the ever-evolving world of cybersecurity.

CHAPTER 4: EXPLOITATION TECHNIQUES

ADVANCED EXPLOITS AND PAYLOADS

Welcome to the world of advanced exploitation techniques. In this chapter, we will explore how ethical hackers go beyond the basics and dive into advanced exploits and payloads. Our focus is on practical instructions and insights to help you understand and implement these techniques effectively without diving into the intricacies of code.

The Role of Advanced Exploits and Payloads

Advanced exploits and payloads are fundamental in ethical hacking. They empower ethical hackers to move beyond simple vulnerabilities and gain a more profound understanding of a target system's security. Let's understand the significance of these techniques:

1. **Maximized Impact**:

    - Advanced exploits enable ethical hackers to exploit complex vulnerabilities, potentially gaining full control over a target system. This allows for a deeper and more comprehensive assessment of the target's security posture.

2. **Customization**:

- Advanced payloads are highly customizable, allowing ethical hackers to tailor their attacks to specific target systems. This customization significantly increases the likelihood of success.

3. **Persistence**:

- Some advanced payloads are designed to maintain access to a compromised system, ensuring that ethical hackers can continue their assessments and gather more information over time.

4. **In-Depth Assessment**:

- Using advanced exploits and payloads, ethical hackers can uncover vulnerabilities that might be missed with basic techniques. This provides a more thorough and nuanced assessment of the target's security.

Let's now embark on a practical journey of working with advanced exploits and payloads.

Practical Steps: Advanced Exploits

1. **Identify Vulnerabilities**:

   - Begin by identifying vulnerabilities in your target system. This involves conducting thorough scans using tools like Nmap to find open ports and services.

2. **Research Known Vulnerabilities**:

   - Research known vulnerabilities associated with the services and software running on the target system. Valuable resources like the Common Vulnerabilities and Exposures (CVE) database can help you in this regard.

3. **Select an Appropriate Exploit**:

   - Choose an exploit that matches the identified vulnerability and suits the target system. Numerous exploit databases and repositories are available to help you find suitable exploits.

4. **Customize the Exploit**:

- Modify the exploit to match the specific characteristics of the target system. Ensure that parameters, such as the target IP and port, are accurately configured.

5. **Execute the Exploit**:

   - Run the exploit and closely observe the results. Be prepared to analyze error messages or unexpected behavior. A successful exploit may grant you access to the target system.

PRACTICAL STEPS: ADVANCED PAYLOADS

1. **Define Your Objectives**:

   - Before utilizing an advanced payload, clearly define your objectives. What do you aim to achieve? It could be gaining control of the target system, maintaining access, or collecting specific data.

2. **Select the Appropriate Payload**:

   - Choose a payload that aligns with your objectives. Consider factors such as the target system, its operating system, and the level of access you wish to obtain.

3. **Payload Customization**:

- Customize the payload to match the target system's characteristics. This may involve configuring parameters like the target IP, port, and payload type.

4. **Payload Delivery**:

- Decide on the method you will use to deliver the payload to the target system. Options include email attachments, malicious websites, or other delivery mechanisms.

5. **Execute the Payload**:

- Execute the payload according to your plan. Be ready to monitor the results and maintain access if that's part of your objectives.

Mastering advanced exploits and payloads is a significant milestone in your ethical hacking journey. These techniques enable you to delve deeper into target systems, uncover complex vulnerabilities, and maintain access for in-depth assessments. By following these practical steps, you can enhance your ethical hacking skills and provide more comprehensive security assessments to clients and organizations. As we continue our exploration, you'll gain more insights into the dynamic world of cybersecurity.

TAKING CONTROL: REMOTE SYSTEM EXPLOITATION

In the realm of ethical hacking, the ability to remotely exploit a target system is a potent skill. It allows ethical hackers to gain access to and control over a target system from a distance, simulating what malicious actors might attempt. In this section, we'll explore remote system exploitation, focusing on practical steps and insights without diving into extensive code details.

Understanding Remote System Exploitation

Remote system exploitation involves taking control of a target system over a network or the internet. This method of attack is particularly significant because it replicates real-world scenarios where attackers may attempt to compromise systems from afar. Understanding remote exploitation is crucial for ethical hackers as it allows them to:

1. **Assess Realistic Threats**: By mastering remote exploitation, ethical hackers can assess the security posture of a target system under conditions that mimic genuine threats.

2. **Identify Vulnerabilities**: The process of remote exploitation reveals vulnerabilities in network configurations, services, and applications that may be susceptible to attacks.

3. **Simulate Cyberattacks**: Ethical hackers can simulate cyberattacks, helping organizations understand their vulnerabilities and weaknesses before malicious actors do.

4. **Enhance Security Measures**: Through remote exploitation, organizations can identify areas where security measures need improvement and take action to bolster their defenses.

Practical Steps: Remote System Exploitation

Here, we'll outline practical steps for conducting remote system exploitation as an ethical hacker:

1. Reconnaissance and Information Gathering

Before attempting remote exploitation, gather information about the target system. Use tools like Nmap to scan for open ports and services. Look for vulnerabilities or known exploits associated with the identified services.

2. Select an Appropriate Exploit

Choose an exploit that matches the identified vulnerability and is suitable for remote exploitation. Make sure it aligns with your ethical hacking objectives.

3. Payload Customization

Customize the payload to suit the target system. Ensure that you configure parameters like the target IP address and port correctly.

4. Payload Delivery

Determine how you will deliver the payload to the target system remotely. Methods can include email attachments, malicious websites, or other network-based delivery mechanisms.

5. Execution and Gaining Access

Execute the payload and observe the results. If successful, you should gain remote access to the target system. This access allows you to control the system as needed for your assessment.

6. MAINTAINING ACCESS (Optional)

In some cases, maintaining access to the compromised system is vital. Consider implementing methods that allow you to re-establish control if your initial access is lost.

7. Objective Achievement

Ensure that you achieve the objectives set for your ethical hacking engagement. This may involve demonstrating the potential impact of a successful exploit, accessing specific data, or showcasing system weaknesses.

8. Document Findings

Thorough documentation is a fundamental aspect of ethical hacking. Record the details of the remote system exploitation, including the identified vulnerability, the exploit used, and the impact on the target system.

9. Recommend Mitigation

Provide recommendations for mitigating the identified vulnerabilities and enhancing the security of the target system. Your insights should support security improvements.

Key Considerations for Ethical Hackers

While remote system exploitation is a valuable skill, it's crucial for ethical hackers to adhere to specific principles and guidelines:

1. Legal and Ethical Compliance

Sql Copy code

Ensure that your actions comply with local and international laws.

2. Permission and Scope

Sql Copy code

Always operate within the defined scope of your ethical hacking engagement. Confirm that your actions are authorized and aligned with the objectives.

3. Data Privacy

Sql Copy code

Respect data privacy regulations, especially when dealing with systems that may contain sensitive or personal information.

4. Documentation

Vbnet Copy code

Maintain detailed records of your activities, findings, and recommendations. This documentation is crucial for clients and organizations to take necessary actions.

5. Continuous Learning

C sharp Copy code

Ethical hacking is an ever-evolving field. Stay updated with the latest trends, vulnerabilities, and exploitation techniques.

Conclusion

Remote system exploitation is a critical skill for ethical hackers, enabling them to assess and replicate real-world threats to target systems. By following these practical steps and focusing on the objectives of ethical hacking engagements, you can effectively conduct remote system exploitation and provide valuable insights to clients and organizations. As we progress further in this journey, you'll delve into more advanced aspects of ethical hacking and cybersecurity. Remember to always act responsibly, ethically, and within the bounds of the law while honing your ethical hacking skills.

CHAPTER 5: PRIVILEGE ESCALATION

Elevating Your Access Privileges

Welcome to the world of privilege escalation in the realm of ethical hacking. In this chapter, we'll explore the techniques and strategies that allow ethical hackers to elevate their access privileges on target systems. Privilege escalation is a critical skill for ethical hackers as it enables them to understand and exploit vulnerabilities that may grant them higher levels of access and control over a system.

UNDERSTANDING PRIVILEGE ESCALATION

Privilege escalation involves the process of gaining higher access privileges than initially granted to a user. It is a crucial concept in ethical hacking as it allows hackers to uncover and exploit weaknesses in a system's security. Understanding privilege escalation is vital because it enables ethical hackers to:

1. **Assess the Full Scope**: By mastering privilege escalation, ethical hackers can assess a target system comprehensively, understanding the extent of their access and control.

2. **Uncover Hidden Vulnerabilities**: The process of privilege escalation often reveals hidden vulnerabilities that may not be apparent at lower privilege levels.

3. **Simulate Advanced Attacks**: Ethical hackers can simulate sophisticated attacks where malicious actors attempt to gain elevated access to a system.

4. **Enhance Security Measures**: Through privilege escalation testing, organizations can identify and address weaknesses that could lead to unauthorized access.

Practical Steps: Privilege Escalation

Here, we'll outline practical steps for conducting privilege escalation as an ethical hacker:

1. Initial Access Assessment

Begin by assessing your initial level of access to the target system. Understand the privileges and limitations associated with your current user or account.

2. Reconnaissance

Conduct reconnaissance to identify potential vulnerabilities that could lead to privilege escalation. This may involve scanning the system for misconfigurations, known vulnerabilities, or weak access controls.

3. Exploitation

Select an appropriate exploitation method or technique based on the identified vulnerabilities. This could include exploiting misconfigured permissions, leveraging known vulnerabilities, or using social engineering tactics.

4. Privilege Elevation

Execute the chosen exploitation method to escalate your access privileges. This may involve gaining administrative or root-level access to the system.

5. Objective Achievement

Ensure that you achieve the objectives set for your ethical hacking engagement. This may include demonstrating the potential impact of privilege escalation, accessing specific data, or showcasing system weaknesses.

6. Documentation

Thoroughly document your privilege escalation activities, including the identified vulnerabilities, the methods used, and the extent of elevated access achieved.

7. Recommendations for Mitigation

Provide recommendations for mitigating the identified vulnerabilities and enhancing the security of the target system. Your insights should support security improvements.

ETHICAL HACKING PRINCIPLES

While privilege escalation is a powerful skill, ethical hackers must adhere to specific principles and guidelines:

1. Legal Compliance

Ensure that your actions comply with local and international laws.

2. Authorized Scope

Always operate within the defined scope of your ethical hacking engagement. Confirm that your actions are authorized and aligned with the objectives.

3. Data Privacy

Respect data privacy regulations, especially when dealing with systems that may contain sensitive or personal information.

4. Transparency and Accountability

Maintain transparency in your actions and be accountable for your findings and recommendations.

5. Continuous Learning

Stay updated with the latest privilege escalation techniques and security trends to ensure you remain effective in your role as an ethical hacker.

Privilege escalation is a fundamental aspect of ethical hacking, enabling hackers to assess and exploit vulnerabilities that grant them higher levels of access to target systems. By following these practical steps and adhering to ethical hacking principles, you can effectively conduct privilege escalation assessments and provide valuable insights to clients and organizations. As we continue our journey in the world of ethical hacking, you'll explore more advanced techniques and concepts that will further enhance your skills in cybersecurity.

GAINING ROOT: ADVANCED TECHNIQUES

In the realm of ethical hacking, gaining root access to a system is often considered the pinnacle of privilege escalation. Root access, also known as superuser access or administrative privileges, provides the highest level of control and authority over a system. This level of access allows an individual to make critical changes, access sensitive data, and effectively take over the system. However, obtaining root access is no simple task and requires advanced techniques and strategies.

The Significance of Root Access

Root access, or equivalent administrative privileges on non-Linux systems, is the highest level of access that a user can attain on a Unix-based operating system. In the context of ethical hacking, gaining root access is a significant achievement for several reasons:

1. **Full System Control**: Root access grants control over every aspect of the system, from user accounts to system configurations. This level of control is essential for thorough security assessments.

2. **Access to Sensitive Data**: Root access provides the ability to access sensitive data, including confidential files, databases, and user information, which is invaluable for evaluating security measures.

3. **Executing System-Level Commands**: Root users can execute system-level commands, making it easier to explore and manipulate system resources, processes, and services.

4. **Unrestricted Modification**: Administrative privileges allow for unrestricted modification of system files, configurations, and settings, providing insight into potential vulnerabilities.

5. **Higher Impact Demonstrations**: Gaining root access allows ethical hackers to demonstrate the most severe consequences of a security breach to clients or organizations, emphasizing the importance of security measures.

ADVANCED TECHNIQUES FOR GAINING ROOT ACCESS

Gaining root access typically involves exploiting vulnerabilities, misconfigurations, or weaknesses in the target system. Advanced techniques for obtaining root access require in-depth knowledge of operating systems, exploitation methods, and a keen understanding of the system's security landscape. Here are some advanced techniques for gaining root access:

1. Kernel Exploitation:

Vbnet Copy code

Kernel exploits target vulnerabilities in the operating system's kernel, which is the core component responsible for managing system resources. These exploits can provide an attacker with elevated privileges, including root access. They often involve techniques like buffer overflows, race conditions, and memory corruption.

2. Privilege Escalation Vulnerabilities:

Sql Copy code

Privilege escalation vulnerabilities, also known as "privilege escalation exploits," are specific weaknesses that, when exploited, allow an attacker to escalate their privileges to the root level. These vulnerabilities can exist in system services, applications, or configuration settings.

3. SUID and SGID Exploitation:

Vbnet Copy code

Set-User-ID (SUID) and Set-Group-ID (SGID) permissions on files can be exploited to gain elevated privileges. When an SUID or SGID binary is executed, it runs with the permissions of the file owner or group owner, respectively. Attackers can take advantage of these permissions to execute code with elevated privileges.

4. Script and Configuration Flaws:

Sql Copy code

Poorly configured scripts or system configurations can provide avenues for privilege escalation. Ethical hackers may identify weaknesses in scripts, cron jobs, or system configurations that allow them to execute commands with root-level privileges.

5. Password Cracking and Brute-Force Attacks:

Csharp Copy code

In some cases, gaining root access may involve cracking passwords or performing brute-force attacks on authentication mechanisms. This is often a last resort when other methods have failed, and it requires extensive knowledge of password security.

6. Social Engineering:

Vbnet Copy code

Social engineering techniques can be employed to manipulate individuals with administrative access into disclosing critical information or providing access to the root account. This could involve tactics like phishing, impersonation, or psychological manipulation.

7. Zero-Day Exploits:

Css Copy code

A zero-day exploit targets vulnerabilities that are not yet known to the software vendor or the security community. These exploits are highly valuable because they provide a window of opportunity to gain root access before a patch is developed.

ROOTKITS AND PRIVILEGE ESCALATION TOOLS

Vbnet Copy code

Rootkits and specialized privilege escalation tools are designed to maintain unauthorized access to a system with root privileges. Once root access is obtained, these tools can be used to ensure continued control.

Ethical Considerations

Gaining root access as an ethical hacker comes with significant responsibilities and ethical considerations. Ethical hackers must always operate within the legal boundaries of their engagements and adhere to strict ethical guidelines. Here are some key ethical considerations:

1. **Authorized Access**: Root access should only be pursued within the scope of an authorized engagement,

with explicit permission from the system owner or organization.

2. **Data Privacy**: Respect data privacy regulations and handle sensitive information with care.

3. **Transparency**: Maintain transparency in your actions, and always be prepared to explain and justify your activities to stakeholders.

4. **Documentation**: Thoroughly document your actions, findings, and any vulnerabilities discovered during the privilege escalation process.

5. **Disclosure**: When vulnerabilities are discovered, ethical hackers should follow responsible disclosure practices to ensure that the system owner can take appropriate actions to secure their system.

Gaining root access is a significant milestone in the world of ethical hacking. It requires advanced techniques, a deep understanding of system vulnerabilities, and a commitment to ethical principles. Ethical hackers who aim to gain root access must always operate within the boundaries of legal and ethical guidelines, ensuring that their actions contribute to the enhancement of cybersecurity and the protection of systems and data.

CHAPTER 6: POST-EXPLOITATION MASTERY

Stealthy Persistence and Covering Tracks

Welcome to the world of post-exploitation mastery, a phase of ethical hacking where you transition from gaining initial access to maintaining access, extracting valuable data, and covering your tracks. In this chapter, we will delve into the techniques and strategies ethical hackers use during post-exploitation activities, without delving into extensive code details.

THE SIGNIFICANCE OF POST-EXPLOITATION

Post-exploitation is a critical phase in ethical hacking, as it allows you to:

1. **Maintain Access**: Ensure that you can revisit the compromised system and maintain control as necessary, even after the initial breach.

2. **Data Extraction**: Retrieve valuable data and information from the target system, which is crucial for security assessments and reporting.

3. **Stealthy Persistence**: Avoid detection by the system's administrators or security measures, enabling prolonged access for thorough assessments.

4. **Cover Tracks**: Erase or manipulate evidence of your presence on the compromised system to maintain anonymity and reduce the risk of exposure.

POST-EXPLOITATION TECHNIQUES

1. Privilege Escalation and Persistence:

After gaining initial access, ethical hackers often seek to maintain access by establishing backdoors or creating new accounts with elevated privileges. This ensures that they can re-enter the system as needed.

2. Rootkits and Trojans:

Rootkits and trojans are malicious tools used to maintain access and control over a system. Rootkits are designed to hide their presence, while trojans can provide remote control.

3. Steganography:

Steganography involves hiding data within other non-suspicious data. Ethical hackers can use steganography to exfiltrate sensitive information without arousing suspicion.

4. Data Encryption:

When extracting sensitive data, encrypting it before exfiltration ensures that even if intercepted, the data remains confidential and secure.

5. Data Exfiltration Techniques:

Ethical hackers may employ various data exfiltration techniques, such as email, cloud storage, or file transfer protocols, to move data from the compromised system to their control.

Covering Tracks

Covering your tracks during post-exploitation is essential to maintain stealth and prevent detection by system administrators and security personnel. Some techniques include:

1. Log Manipulation:

Alter or delete log entries that may reveal your activities on the compromised system. This includes event logs, access logs, and system logs.

2. File Timestamp Alteration:

Modify file timestamps to create false trail or obfuscate the timeline of your activities.

3. User Account Cleanup:

Remove or manipulate user accounts and permissions to eliminate evidence of your presence.

4. Removal of Malicious Tools:

Eradicate any tools or scripts used during the exploitation phase to reduce the risk of detection.

5. File Deletion and Shredding:

Delete or shred files that contain sensitive data or may reveal your actions on the system.

6. Antiforensic Tools:

Some ethical hackers employ antiforensic tools to actively counter forensic analysis attempts.

Ethical Considerations

In the post-exploitation phase, ethical hackers face specific ethical considerations:

1. **Legitimate Authorization**: Ensure that post-exploitation activities are conducted within the bounds

of authorized assessments and in compliance with relevant laws and regulations.

2. **Data Privacy**: Handle sensitive data responsibly, respecting privacy regulations and security measures.

3. **Transparency**: If your activities are detected, be prepared to engage transparently with system administrators or security personnel to explain your presence and objectives.

4. **Legal Boundaries**: Understand and respect legal boundaries related to post-exploitation activities, especially when interacting with systems in various jurisdictions.

DATA EXTRACTION AND EXFILTRATION

The second component of post-exploitation involves the extraction and exfiltration of valuable data from the compromised system. Data extraction techniques include:

1. Data Identification:

Identify and locate the data that is of interest or relevance to your ethical hacking objectives. This may include sensitive files, databases, or configurations.

2. Data Compression:

Compress data to reduce the size of files before exfiltration. This can be helpful in optimizing the transfer process and evading detection.

3. Secure Data Transfer:

Employ secure data transfer methods to ensure that the exfiltrated data remains confidential during transit. Encrypted connections, secure protocols, and VPNs can enhance security.

4. Stealthy Exfiltration:

Use covert techniques to exfiltrate data, such as disguising data in non-suspicious traffic or transferring it during low-activity periods to minimize detection risk.

5. Data Handling and Storage:

Securely store and manage the exfiltrated data, ensuring it is protected and confidential throughout the post-exploitation phase.

Conclusion

Mastering post-exploitation activities is a crucial aspect of ethical hacking. It allows you to not only gain access but also maintain it, extract valuable data, and cover your tracks effectively. The ethical considerations surrounding post-exploitation are paramount, and ethical hackers must operate within legal boundaries and with the utmost respect for privacy and security regulations. As you progress further in your ethical hacking journey, you'll continue to explore advanced techniques and concepts that will enhance your skills in cybersecurity.

CHAPTER 7: WIRELESS HACKING

ADVANCED WI-FI EXPLOITS AND ATTACKS

Welcome to the world of wireless hacking, where the vulnerabilities of Wi-Fi networks are explored and exploited. In this chapter, we will delve into advanced Wi-Fi exploits and attacks used by ethical hackers. We'll focus on understanding the techniques and strategies, without going into extensive code details.

SIGNIFICANCE OF WIRELESS HACKING

Wireless hacking plays a crucial role in ethical hacking, as it allows you to:

1. **Assess Network Security**: Evaluate the security of Wi-Fi networks to identify vulnerabilities that could be exploited by malicious actors.

2. **Access Control**: Test access control measures to ensure that only authorized devices can connect to the network.

3. **Data Protection**: Examine encryption and data protection mechanisms to prevent unauthorized access to sensitive information.

4. **Security Awareness**: Raise awareness among organizations and individuals about the importance of securing Wi-Fi networks.

ADVANCED WI-FI EXPLOITS AND ATTACKS

1. Deauthentication and Disassociation Attacks:

These attacks target the disconnection of devices from a Wi-Fi network by sending deauthentication or disassociation frames. This technique can disrupt network access and create opportunities for further attacks.

2. Evil Twin Access Points:

Ethical hackers create rogue access points with the same name as legitimate networks, luring unsuspecting users to connect. Once connected, the hacker can intercept traffic or launch attacks.

3. Rogue Devices and MAC Spoofing:

This technique involves impersonating legitimate devices or spoofing MAC addresses to gain unauthorized access to Wi-Fi networks.

4. Packet Sniffing and Analysis:

Ethical hackers use tools to capture and analyze Wi-Fi traffic, identifying potential vulnerabilities or insecure data transmissions.

5. Password Attacks:

Ethical hackers may employ techniques like dictionary attacks, brute-force attacks, and rainbow tables to crack Wi-Fi network passwords.

6. Man-in-the-Middle (MitM) Attacks:

MitM attacks intercept and potentially manipulate communications between devices and the network. This can expose sensitive information or lead to other attacks.

7. WPS Exploits:

Attacks against Wi-Fi Protected Setup (WPS) can reveal PINs or credentials to gain unauthorized access to a network.

8. Encryption Weaknesses:

Ethical hackers examine encryption protocols, such as WEP, WPA, and WPA2, to uncover vulnerabilities and weaknesses that may allow unauthorized access.

Cracking WPA/WPA2 Passphrases

1. Capture the Handshake:

To crack WPA/WPA2 passphrases, you first need to capture the four-way handshake that occurs when a device connects to the network. Tools like Wireshark can help capture this handshake.

2. Wordlist Attacks:

Wordlist attacks involve using a list of potential passphrases to attempt to crack the captured handshake. Tools like Aircrack-ng or Hashcat can be used for this purpose.

3. Brute-Force Attacks:

Brute-force attacks involve trying all possible combinations of characters until the correct passphrase is found. These attacks are time-consuming and require substantial computing power.

4. Dictionary Attacks:

Dictionary attacks use a predefined list of words and phrases to attempt to crack the passphrase. This approach is more efficient than brute-force attacks.

5. Rainbow Tables:

Rainbow tables are precomputed tables of hashed passphrases that can be used to quickly look up the original passphrase when cracking hashes. This method can be faster than traditional attacks.

Ethical Considerations

Wireless hacking, like other areas of ethical hacking, comes with ethical considerations:

1. **Legal Authorization**: Always conduct wireless hacking within the scope of authorized engagements and in compliance with relevant laws and regulations.

2. **Data Privacy**: Handle any data captured or accessed with care and respect data privacy regulations.

3. **Transparency**: If your activities are detected, be prepared to engage transparently with network administrators or security personnel to explain your presence and objectives.

4. **Responsible Disclosure**: When vulnerabilities are discovered, ethical hackers should follow responsible disclosure practices to ensure that the network owner can take appropriate actions to secure their network.

Conclusion

Wireless hacking is an essential aspect of ethical hacking that allows ethical hackers to identify vulnerabilities and weaknesses in Wi-Fi networks. The ethical considerations surrounding wireless hacking are paramount, and ethical hackers must operate within legal boundaries and with the utmost respect for privacy and security regulations. As you continue your journey in ethical hacking, you'll explore advanced techniques and concepts that enhance your skills in cybersecurity.

CHAPTER 8: WEB APPLICATION HACKING

MASTERING WEB VULNERABILITIES

Welcome to the world of web application hacking, a domain where the vulnerabilities of web-based applications are uncovered and exploited. In this chapter, we will explore the art of mastering web vulnerabilities, understanding various techniques and strategies employed by ethical hackers to assess, expose, and mitigate web application security issues.

The Importance of Web Application Hacking

Web applications are a fundamental part of the digital landscape, serving as the interface between users and data. Ensuring the security of web applications is essential as they often deal with sensitive information. Ethical hackers delve into web application hacking for several reasons:

1. **Security Assessment**: Ethical hackers scrutinize web applications to discover vulnerabilities that malicious actors could exploit. This allows organizations to strengthen their security measures.

2. **Protection of Data**: Unauthorized access to web applications can lead to data breaches, causing financial and reputational damage. Ethical hacking helps safeguard sensitive information.

3. **User Privacy**: Protecting user data and privacy is paramount. Ethical hackers aim to identify and eliminate vulnerabilities that could compromise these aspects.

4. **Regulatory Compliance**: Many industries have regulatory requirements regarding the security of web applications. Ethical hacking ensures compliance with these regulations.

Mastering Web Vulnerabilities

SQL Injection (SQLi)

SQL injection is a widespread vulnerability that allows attackers to manipulate a web application's database by injecting malicious SQL queries. Ethical hackers use various techniques to identify and mitigate SQLi vulnerabilities.

Cross-Site Scripting (XSS)

Ethical hackers discover and fix these issues to prevent the execution of harmful scripts.

Cross-Site Request Forgery (CSRF)

CSRF attacks trick users into performing actions without their consent when they are logged into a web application. Ethical hackers assess and counter these vulnerabilities to protect user actions.

Insecure Deserialization

Insecure deserialization vulnerabilities can lead to remote code execution. Ethical hackers scrutinize these issues to prevent malicious actors from exploiting them.

Broken Authentication:

Broken authentication vulnerabilities can enable attackers to impersonate users and gain unauthorized access. Ethical hackers work to identify and rectify these vulnerabilities.

Security Misconfigurations:

Misconfigurations can expose sensitive information or provide unauthorized access to parts of a web application. Ethical hackers help organizations correct these issues.

BYPASSING WEB APPLICATION FIREWALLS

Session Management Bypass:

Ethical hackers may attempt to manipulate session management mechanisms to gain unauthorized access to user accounts or administrative interfaces.

WAF EVASION TECHNIQUES

Techniques such as encoding, obfuscation, and evasion can be used to bypass Web Application Firewalls (WAFs) to conduct attacks against web applications.

EXPLOITING KNOWN WAF VULNERABILITIES

Some WAFs may have known vulnerabilities or misconfigurations that can be exploited. Ethical hackers investigate these weaknesses to assess the security of web applications.

Bypassing Rate Limiting and Authentication Controls

By cleverly circumventing rate limiting and authentication mechanisms, ethical hackers can assess the resilience of web applications to abuse and unauthorized access.

File Upload Vulnerabilities:

Some web applications allow file uploads. Ethical hackers may find ways to upload malicious files or scripts to exploit vulnerabilities.

Cookie Manipulation:

Cookie-based attacks can involve stealing or manipulating user cookies to gain unauthorized access. Ethical hackers assess these vulnerabilities to enhance security.

Ethical Considerations

Web application hacking comes with ethical considerations:

1. **Legal Authorization**: Ensure that web application hacking activities are conducted within the scope of authorized assessments and comply with relevant laws and regulations.

2. **Data Privacy**: Handle any data captured or accessed with care, respecting data privacy regulations.

3. **Transparency**: If your activities are detected, be prepared to engage transparently with web application owners or security personnel to explain your presence and objectives.

4. **Responsible Disclosure**: When vulnerabilities are discovered, ethical hackers should follow responsible disclosure practices, allowing web application owners to take appropriate actions to secure their applications.

Conclusion

Mastering web vulnerabilities and bypassing Web Application Firewalls is a crucial aspect of ethical hacking. It empowers ethical hackers to assess and fortify web application security, ensuring the protection of user data, privacy, and regulatory compliance. The ethical considerations surrounding web application hacking are paramount, and ethical hackers must operate within legal boundaries and with the utmost respect for privacy and security regulations. As you continue your journey in ethical hacking, you'll explore advanced techniques and concepts that enhance your skills in cybersecurity.

CHAPTER 9: EVADING DETECTION

Welcome to the world of evading detection, a chapter that delves into advanced techniques to operate in the shadows, avoiding detection by security measures and forensic investigations. In this chapter, we will explore the methods ethical hackers employ to stay hidden and maintain a low profile, providing step-by-step instructions and real-world examples.

The Importance of Evading Detection

Evading detection is crucial for ethical hackers as it allows them to:

1. **Uncover Vulnerabilities**: Ethical hackers need to assess security measures and systems without raising alarm, ensuring they can uncover vulnerabilities effectively.

2. **Mitigate Security Risks**: By avoiding detection, ethical hackers can identify security risks and address them before malicious actors exploit them.

3. **Responsible Disclosure**: Operating discreetly allows ethical hackers to responsibly disclose vulnerabilities to organizations without causing undue panic or damage.

4. **Penetration Testing**: In the context of penetration testing, staying under the radar ensures that the test reflects real-world conditions and responses to potential threats.

ADVANCED TECHNIQUES TO STAY UNDER THE RADAR

1. Port Scanning Techniques:

Port scanning is an essential part of network reconnaissance. Advanced techniques like slow scanning, idle scanning, and decoy scanning can help ethical hackers scan targets discreetly. **Example**: Utilizing the Nmap tool for a slow scan with a command like `nmap -T2 -sS target.com` to minimize the chance of detection.

2. Stealthy Payload Delivery:

When delivering payloads, ethical hackers use various techniques to evade detection. Examples include encoding payloads, using encrypted communication channels, or employing steganography to hide malicious code within innocent-looking data. **Example**: Employing Base64 encoding to obfuscate a payload before delivery.

3. Hiding in Plain Sight:

Ethical hackers can use techniques like blending with normal traffic, using proxy chains, or employing covert channels to maintain a low profile. **Example**: Utilizing a proxy chain with multiple proxy servers to obfuscate the origin of network traffic.

4. Evasion Techniques in Exploits:

When exploiting vulnerabilities, ethical hackers employ evasion techniques like avoiding known patterns, implementing custom shellcode, and modifying exploits to bypass security measures. **Example**: Customizing an exploit to evade intrusion detection systems (IDS) by altering the payload structure.

5. Payload Exfiltration:

When exfiltrating data, ethical hackers use covert channels, encryption, and protocols that are less likely to be monitored or flagged. **Example**: Employing DNS tunneling to exfiltrate data through DNS queries.

6. Tunneling and Proxy Chains:

Tunneling through protocols like SSH or employing proxy chains can help ethical hackers route traffic discreetly, obscuring their activities. **Example**: Creating an SSH tunnel to route traffic through an intermediate server.

ANTI-FORENSICS AND ANONYMITY

1. Data Sanitization:

Ethical hackers often sanitize data to remove any traces of their presence or activities. This includes removing logs, temporary files, and any artifacts that may have been left behind. **Example**: Using tools like BleachBit to clean temporary files and traces from a system.

2. Encryption and Steganography:

Encryption can protect data from being intercepted and analyzed. Steganography hides data within other non-suspicious data, making it difficult to detect. **Example**: Using GnuPG for email encryption or tools like Steghide for steganography.

3. Anonymity Tools:

Ethical hackers use anonymity tools like Tor, VPNs, and proxy servers to obfuscate their online activities and maintain anonymity. **Example**: Configuring the Tor browser for anonymous web browsing.

4. Secure Communication:

Ethical hackers employ encrypted communication methods to protect their conversations and data during penetration testing or ethical hacking engagements. **Example**: Using Signal or Wire for end-to-end encrypted communication.

5. Anti-Forensic Tools:

Tools designed for anti-forensics can help ethical hackers cover their tracks by modifying or erasing evidence of their activities. **Example**: Using tools like Timestomp to modify file timestamps.

Ethical Considerations

While evading detection is a critical aspect of ethical hacking, it is accompanied by ethical considerations:

1. **Legal Authorization**: Ensure that activities are conducted within the scope of authorized assessments and comply with relevant laws and regulations.

2. **Data Privacy**: Respect data privacy regulations and handle sensitive information with care.

3. **Transparency**: If your activities are detected, be prepared to engage transparently with system administrators or security personnel to explain your presence and objectives.

4. **Responsible Disclosure**: When vulnerabilities are discovered, follow responsible disclosure practices, allowing organizations to take appropriate actions to secure their systems.

Conclusion

Staying under the radar and evading detection is a vital aspect of ethical hacking. It enables ethical hackers to assess and mitigate security risks discreetly, protect data privacy, and responsibly disclose vulnerabilities. The ethical considerations surrounding evading detection are essential, and ethical hackers must operate within legal boundaries and respect privacy and security regulations. As you continue your journey in ethical hacking, these advanced techniques will enhance your skills in cybersecurity.

CHAPTER 10: ETHICAL HACKING BEST PRACTICES

The Code of Ethics: Staying on the Right Side

In the world of ethical hacking, the importance of adhering to a strong code of ethics cannot be overstated. This chapter explores the fundamental principles that guide ethical hackers, as well as the legal implications and responsible practices that ensure ethical hacking remains on the right side of the law and morality.

The Code of Ethics for Ethical Hackers

Ethical hacking, like any profession, is guided by a code of ethics that helps practitioners make sound and morally upright decisions. The primary components of the ethical hacker's code of ethics include:

LEGITIMATE AUTHORIZATION

Ethical hackers must always operate within the bounds of authorized assessments. This means they should only test systems and networks with explicit permission from the owners.

User Privacy and Data Protection

Ethical hackers must take every precaution to protect user privacy and sensitive data. This includes refraining from viewing, disclosing, or tampering with sensitive information without explicit consent.

Transparency and Informed Consent

Whenever possible, ethical hackers should maintain transparency about their activities. In cases where covert or stealthy testing is required, the hacker must obtain informed consent from the organization.

Responsible Disclosure:

When vulnerabilities are identified, ethical hackers should follow responsible disclosure practices. This includes notifying the organization about the issues discovered and providing them with sufficient time to address and remediate the vulnerabilities.

Legal Compliance:

Ethical hackers must always operate within the bounds of the law and adhere to relevant regulations and statutes. Unauthorized access, data theft, or any illegal activities are strictly prohibited.

Continual Professional Development:

Ethical hackers should engage in continuous learning and professional development to stay updated with the latest security trends, tools, and techniques. This ensures their skills are relevant and effective.

Legal Implications of Ethical Hacking

The legal landscape surrounding ethical hacking can be complex, and ethical hackers must be aware of the potential legal implications of their actions. Key legal considerations include:

1. Authorization and Consent:

The foremost legal requirement is obtaining proper authorization and consent for penetration testing or security assessments. Unauthorized testing can lead to legal repercussions.

2. Data Privacy Laws:

Ethical hackers must comply with data privacy laws, which vary by jurisdiction. Handling and safeguarding user data must be in alignment with these regulations.

3. Computer Fraud and Abuse Act (CFAA):

In the United States, the Computer Fraud and Abuse Act is a federal law that governs computer-related activities. Ethical hackers should be familiar with this law and ensure their actions remain within its bounds.

4. International Laws and Treaties:

Ethical hackers operating internationally must be aware of laws, treaties, and agreements that affect their activities across borders. Cybercrime legislation and international cooperation agreements are relevant here.

5. Contractual Agreements:

Contracts and service-level agreements (SLAs) with organizations may specify the rules and legal obligations regarding ethical hacking engagements. Ethical hackers should review these documents carefully.

6. Legal Protection and Legal Advisors:

Ethical hackers should consider seeking legal advice to navigate the legal complexities surrounding their activities. Legal protection and advice can be invaluable.

RESPONSIBLE HACKING PRACTICES

Responsible hacking practices are crucial for ensuring that ethical hacking is conducted in a professional, secure, and effective manner. Some of the best practices include:

1. Documentation:

Keeping thorough records of all activities, findings, communications, and reports is essential. Proper documentation ensures transparency and accountability.

2. Risk Assessment:

Before initiating any engagement, ethical hackers should conduct a risk assessment to understand potential consequences and prepare accordingly.

3. Communication:

Effective and clear communication with the organization is vital. Discuss the scope, objectives, and constraints of the engagement to ensure mutual understanding.

4. Security of Tools and Data:

Ethical hackers must ensure the security of their tools and data. This includes protecting testing environments, isolating networks, and securely storing findings.

5. Reporting and Remediation:

After identifying vulnerabilities, ethical hackers should provide comprehensive reports to the organization, including detailed explanations, potential impacts, and recommendations for remediation.

6. Professionalism:

Ethical hackers should conduct themselves professionally and maintain a high level of integrity in all interactions with the organization and its personnel.

Ethical Hacking Certification and Regulation

To further professionalize the field of ethical hacking, various certifications and regulations have been established. These include:

1. Certified Ethical Hacker (CEH):

Offered by the EC-Council, the CEH certification is a recognized qualification for ethical hackers. It covers various aspects of ethical hacking and information security.

2. Certified Information Systems Security Professional (CISSP):

The CISSP certification is administered by (ISC)² and is a globally recognized credential for information security professionals.

3. Regulatory Bodies and Standards:

Various regulatory bodies and standards, such as ISO/IEC 27001 and the National Institute of Standards and Technology (NIST), provide guidelines and frameworks for information security.

Ethical hacking is a profession that demands a commitment to a strong code of ethics, an understanding of the legal landscape, and the practice of responsible hacking. By adhering to the ethical hacker's code of ethics, respecting legal boundaries, and following responsible hacking practices, ethical hackers can ensure that their activities are conducted with the highest level of professionalism, integrity, and effectiveness. As the field of ethical hacking continues to evolve, these principles remain essential in the quest for a more secure digital world.

THE ROLE OF ETHICAL HACKING IN CYBERSECURITY

Ethical hacking plays a pivotal role in the ever-evolving field of cybersecurity. In this subsection, we will explore the significance of ethical hacking in safeguarding digital ecosystems and how ethical hackers contribute to identifying and mitigating security risks.

Identifying Vulnerabilities Before the Bad Actors

One of the primary functions of ethical hacking is to proactively identify vulnerabilities and security weaknesses before malicious actors can exploit them. By conducting systematic assessments, ethical hackers help organizations uncover potential entry points, weak links, and misconfigurations in their systems and networks.

Vulnerability Assessment and Penetration Testing (VAPT)

Vulnerability assessments and penetration tests are core components of ethical hacking. These practices involve:

1. **Scanning for Weaknesses**: Ethical hackers scan networks, applications, and systems to identify vulnerabilities, misconfigurations, and areas susceptible to exploitation.

2. **Exploitation Simulation**: Through penetration testing, ethical hackers attempt to exploit identified vulnerabilities in a controlled environment to understand their potential impact.

3. **Security Posture Evaluation**: Ethical hackers assess the overall security posture of an organization, providing valuable insights into areas requiring attention.

Benefits of Proactive Vulnerability Discovery

Ethical hacking offers several key benefits:

- **Reduced Risk**: Identifying vulnerabilities before malicious actors do reduces the risk of security breaches and data compromises.

- **Cost Savings**: Addressing vulnerabilities early is more cost-effective than dealing with the aftermath of a security incident.

- **Enhanced Preparedness**: Ethical hacking helps organizations better prepare for security threats and establish robust security measures.

Contributing to Incident Response

Ethical hackers often play an essential role in incident response. When security breaches occur, organizations require skilled professionals who can:

- **Identify Attack Vectors**: Ethical hackers can quickly identify the attack vectors used in security incidents, helping organizations understand how the breach occurred.

- **Forensic Analysis**: Ethical hackers with expertise in digital forensics can assist in the investigation of security incidents, tracing back the steps taken by the attackers.

- **Containment and Remediation**: Ethical hackers can provide recommendations for containing a security incident and remediating the damage.

Post-Incident Ethical Hacking

After a security incident, ethical hackers can help organizations:

- **Analyze the Attack**: Ethical hackers examine the attack methods used and determine how the incident could have been prevented.

- **Patch and Strengthen**: Recommendations from ethical hackers guide organizations in patching vulnerabilities, strengthening security measures, and avoiding similar incidents.

Staying Ahead of Evolving Threats

The cybersecurity landscape is continually evolving, with new threats emerging regularly. Ethical hackers remain at the forefront of this ever-changing battlefield, constantly adapting to new challenges and emerging security risks.

Staying Informed

Ethical hackers must stay informed about:

- **Emerging Threats**: Understanding new attack vectors, malware, and tactics employed by malicious actors is crucial.

- **Security Trends**: Monitoring cybersecurity trends, best practices, and emerging technologies keeps ethical hackers up-to-date.

ADAPTIVE DEFENSES

Ethical hackers often assist organizations in developing adaptive security defenses, which:

- **Utilize Behavioral Analysis**: Advanced security solutions incorporate behavioral analysis to detect anomalies and potential threats.

- **Automate Threat Response**: Automated responses to security incidents help organizations mitigate risks more effectively.

Engaging in Responsible Disclosure

When ethical hackers discover vulnerabilities, they engage in responsible disclosure. This practice involves:

- **Notifying the Affected Parties**: Ethical hackers inform the organization or vendor responsible for the vulnerable system, providing detailed information about the issue.

- **Allowing Time for Remediation**: Ethical hackers give organizations adequate time to address and remediate the vulnerability.

- **Public Disclosure**: If the organization fails to address the issue or the vulnerability poses a significant risk, ethical hackers may choose to disclose the information publicly.

Balancing Transparency and Responsibility

Responsible disclosure is a delicate balance between transparency and responsibility. Ethical hackers aim to protect users, uphold security, and promote responsible vendor behavior.

Conclusion

Ethical hacking is not only a proactive approach to security but also a dynamic field that adapts to emerging threats and vulnerabilities. Ethical hackers play a vital role in protecting digital assets, identifying vulnerabilities before they are exploited, and contributing to incident response and threat detection. Their commitment to responsible disclosure and ethical practices fosters a more secure and resilient digital landscape. As cybersecurity challenges persist, the role of ethical hacking remains indispensable in the ongoing battle to protect digital ecosystems.

CHAPTER 11: REAL-WORLD SCENARIOS

Case Studies and Practical Applications

In this chapter, we delve into the realm of real-world scenarios in ethical hacking. Ethical hacking is not merely a theoretical exercise; it is a practical endeavor that involves solving complex security challenges. We will explore case studies and practical applications of ethical hacking, uncovering the hacking challenges faced and the innovative solutions developed by ethical hackers.

The Practical Nature of Ethical Hacking

Ethical hacking is rooted in practicality, with ethical hackers tasked with addressing real-world security concerns. While theoretical knowledge is essential, the ability to apply this knowledge effectively in practical scenarios is equally critical. Here, we examine the practical applications of ethical hacking through case studies and solutions.

Scenario

A prominent financial institution engaged a team of ethical hackers to perform a comprehensive vulnerability assessment of their network and systems. With the increasing frequency of cyberattacks targeting financial organizations, the institution sought to identify and rectify vulnerabilities before malicious actors could exploit them.

Challenges

COMPLEX NETWORK ARCHITECTURE: The financial institution's network was intricate, comprising multiple branches, data centers, and online banking platforms. Navigating this complex architecture posed a challenge for the ethical hacking team.

- **Regulatory Compliance**: The institution needed to adhere to strict financial regulations and data protection laws. Any vulnerabilities discovered needed to be addressed promptly to maintain compliance.

SOLUTIONS

- **Thorough Scanning**: Ethical hackers employed a combination of network and application scanning tools to identify vulnerabilities. This involved scanning for open ports, services, and web application vulnerabilities.

- **Penetration Testing**: After identifying potential vulnerabilities, the ethical hacking team conducted penetration tests to confirm the feasibility of exploitation. This allowed them to assess the real-world risks associated with the vulnerabilities.

- **Regulatory Compliance Evaluation**: The ethical hackers collaborated with compliance experts to ensure that the vulnerabilities discovered did not violate financial regulations. This involved assessing the impact of the vulnerabilities on regulatory compliance.

Case Study: Insider Threat Investigation

Scenario

A technology company suspected an insider threat within its organization. Unusual system behavior, suspicious access patterns, and data leaks raised concerns about potential unauthorized activities by an employee. The company engaged ethical hackers to investigate the matter.

Challenges

INTERNAL NETWORK MONITORING: Investigating insider threats within an organization's internal network required careful monitoring to identify the source of unauthorized activities.

DATA EXFILTRATION: Identifying and tracking data exfiltration attempts by the insider posed a challenge, as they may have used covert methods to transfer data.

Solutions

- **Network Traffic Analysis**: Ethical hackers utilized network traffic analysis tools to monitor the behavior of the insider, identifying unusual patterns and data transfers.

- **Endpoint Forensics**: In-depth endpoint forensics helped trace the insider's activities on specific devices. This involved examining system logs and user activity.

- **Data Loss Prevention (DLP)**: Ethical hackers implemented DLP solutions to monitor and prevent data exfiltration attempts. This allowed them to detect and block unauthorized data transfers.

Case Study: Red Team Engagement for a Healthcare Provider

Scenario

A healthcare provider sought to assess the resilience of its security measures against external threats. To mimic a real-world cyberattack, they engaged a red team of ethical hackers to perform penetration testing and exploit vulnerabilities, if any, within the organization's security posture.

Challenges

- **Healthcare Data Protection**: The red team needed to test the organization's security without compromising sensitive patient data. This posed a significant challenge in maintaining data privacy.

- **Evasive Techniques**: The red team aimed to employ evasive techniques to bypass security measures without causing disruptions to critical healthcare services.

Solutions

DATA ANONYMIZATION: To protect patient data, the red team anonymized information used in testing, ensuring that no real patient data was at risk.

- **Red Team Scenarios**: The red team used realistic attack scenarios, focusing on techniques that real attackers might use to infiltrate the organization's network.

- **Live Environment Testing**: The red team conducted live testing in a controlled environment to assess the effectiveness of security measures while minimizing potential disruptions.

Real-world scenarios in ethical hacking bring the theoretical knowledge and practical skills of ethical hackers to life. These case studies highlight the complexities and challenges that ethical hackers face when securing organizations against cyber threats. Ethical hackers must navigate intricate network architectures, address insider threats, and mimic real-world attacks, all while adhering to regulatory compliance and data privacy standards. The innovative solutions developed through these scenarios underscore the importance of ethical hacking in protecting digital ecosystems and the continuous evolution of security measures to stay ahead of evolving threats. As you explore the practical applications of ethical hacking in these case studies, you gain valuable insights into the multifaceted nature of this vital field.

CHAPTER 12: STEP BY STEP HOW HACK WITH KALI LINUX

In this chapter, we will explore the profound potential of Kali Linux as a formidable instrument for hacking. With a thorough, step-by-step approach, we will guide aspiring hackers on their journey, starting from the very fundamentals, progressing through each essential step, and culminating in the acquisition of remote access using Kali Linux.

GETTING ACQUAINTED WITH KALI LINUX

Before embarking on your hacking journey, it is essential to become well-versed in your tool of choice. Kali Linux, a specialized operating system designed for ethical hacking, will serve as your faithful companion throughout your ethical hacking exploits. In this subsection, we will explore the fundamentals of Kali Linux, its key features, and how it sets the stage for your journey into the world of ethical hacking.

The Genesis of Kali Linux

Understanding the origin of Kali Linux is the first step in your journey to mastery. Kali Linux emerged as a response to the growing demand for a sophisticated and user-friendly penetration testing platform.

BACKTRACK: The Precursor

Before Kali Linux, there was BackTrack, a popular and comprehensive hacking toolset used by security professionals. BackTrack was celebrated for its extensive collection of hacking tools and its usability. However, it had its limitations, primarily related to keeping up with evolving technology and the need for a more dynamic and advanced platform.

Birth of Kali Linux

In 2013, Kali Linux was born, developed and maintained by Offensive Security. This new operating system aimed to surpass its predecessor, BackTrack, by providing an enhanced platform for ethical hackers, penetration testers, and security enthusiasts.

The Essence of Kali Linux

Kali Linux is not just an operating system; it embodies the essence of ethical hacking. It offers an extensive toolkit that empowers you to test and strengthen the security of networks, systems, and applications. Let's explore the core aspects of Kali Linux that make it the ideal choice for ethical hacking.

A COMPREHENSIVE TOOLSET

Kali Linux boasts an extensive arsenal of over 600 pre-installed tools. These tools are tailored to meet the specific needs of ethical hackers, covering various aspects of information security, vulnerability assessment, network scanning, wireless attacks, and digital forensics, among others.

A Learning Environment

Kali Linux goes beyond being a mere toolbox; it serves as a gateway to the art of ethical hacking. It provides an environment where you can apply your knowledge, explore vulnerabilities, and gain hands-on experience in a safe and controlled setting. It's not just about using tools; it's about developing a profound understanding of the cybersecurity landscape, uncovering vulnerabilities, and learning how to mitigate them.

Continual Updates and Improvements

Kali Linux is committed to continuous improvement. The Kali Linux team maintains a strict update schedule, ensuring that tools are always up-to-date. This dedication guarantees that you're working with the latest and most effective tools available, which is essential in a field that evolves rapidly.

NAVIGATING KALI LINUX

To make the most of Kali Linux, you need to navigate its features and capabilities effectively. The operating system is renowned not only for its technical capabilities but also for its accessibility.

User-Friendly Interface

Kali Linux provides a user-friendly interface, striking a balance between simplicity and functionality. Whether you are a seasoned cybersecurity professional or a newcomer to the field, Kali Linux ensures a smooth journey into the world of ethical hacking.

An Operating System Platform of Choice

Kali Linux is more than just a collection of tools; it is a well-integrated operating system designed for ethical hacking. As you become acquainted with its features, you'll find that Kali Linux offers everything you need to conduct ethical hacking activities effectively.

In the following sections, we will delve deeper into the practical aspects of Kali Linux, guiding you on how to set it up, configure it, and utilize its extensive toolkit for ethical hacking purposes. Your journey into the world of ethical hacking begins with a solid foundation in Kali Linux, and you are well on your way to mastering this powerful tool.

HOW TO START HACKING WITH KALI LINUX

Now that we've had some time to explore Kali Linux and understand why hackers choose this operating system over Windows or Mac for their hacking needs, let's delve into the world of hacking. Specifically, we'll focus on the distinctions between ethical hacking and black hat hacking, which represents the unethical side of hacking.

Before we dig deeper, let's briefly discuss black hat hacking. Black hat hackers are typically the individuals that come to mind when we think about hackers. They have malicious intentions and aim to cause harm. Their activities often involve running illegal businesses, stealing sensitive information, and making money through illicit means. They employ various techniques to achieve their objectives, but the central theme is benefiting themselves at the expense of others.

On the other end of the spectrum, we have ethical hackers. These individuals engage in hacking not to harm others but to protect. They might work for a company to safeguard large corporate networks or apply their skills to secure their own systems. Ethical hackers use similar methods to black hat hackers but with a crucial distinction: they have permission to access the network in question. Unlike black hat hackers, they act within legal and ethical boundaries.

It's important to note that there are various types of hackers with different motivations, knowledge levels, and skills in hacking and coding. However, for now, our focus will remain on understanding the fundamental differences between black hat hackers and ethical hackers.

Let's explore the concept of an Ethical Hacker. Ethical hacking, often referred to as white hat hacking, involves the practice of assessing networks and computer systems to identify and rectify security threats. Ethical hackers undertake these actions with the goal of enhancing security and minimizing potential vulnerabilities.

Ethical hackers, unlike black hat hackers, operate within the boundaries of the law and ethical principles. They aim to assess a system's security by attempting to bypass its defenses and identifying any weak points that malicious hackers could exploit. The knowledge gained from these activities helps organizations improve their system's security, making it less susceptible to potential attacks.

Hacking, in this context, is the process used to discover vulnerabilities within a system. It allows for the identification of entry points, often unauthorized, that malicious actors could use for various illicit activities. It's essential to note that hacking is typically considered illegal, and those caught engaging in illegal hacking activities may face severe consequences.

However, hacking can have legal applications, primarily when conducted with proper authorization. Many companies hire computer experts to assess their systems, searching for vulnerabilities before black hat hackers can exploit them. This proactive approach is a precautionary measure against potentially harmful hacking attempts.

Ethical hackers, often known as white hat hackers, are the individuals engaged in such activities. They conduct ethical hacking, which entails authorized assessments of systems and networks to enhance security.

This distinction leads us to the comparison between white hat and black hat hackers, while recognizing that there are other categories in between. Still, for the purpose of this discussion, we'll primarily focus on understanding the fundamental principles of hacking and its implications.

Now, let's delve into these different types of hackers and the motivations behind their actions.

BLACK HAT HACKERS

When you hear the term "hacker," your initial thoughts might gravitate toward news articles featuring hackers who steal data or engage in unauthorized activities for personal gain. These are the black hat hackers, individuals who infiltrate networks or systems without the owner's permission.

Black hat hackers are driven by personal gain and often employ various techniques to achieve their objectives. They may conduct activities such as man-in-the-middle attacks, keylogging, or other methods to gain unauthorized access and acquire information. Malware, viruses, and Trojan horses are tools they frequently use to breach systems. Successful black hat hacking can result in significant financial losses for companies and damage to their reputation.

WHITE HAT HACKERS

White hat hackers, while possessing similar skills and techniques to black hat hackers, have different motivations. Their intentions are noble, and they always seek proper authorization before assessing a network or system. They may either work on their own network or, as employees of a company, assess their employer's network security.

White hat hackers operate in two primary ways. Firstly, they conduct security assessments to identify vulnerabilities and report them to network administrators or system owners. Secondly, some white hat hackers are genuinely interested in computer systems and work on discovering flaws and vulnerabilities to learn more about the field.

The critical distinction for white hat hackers is that they always have the necessary permissions to access the network. Network administrators or system owners are aware of their presence and their purpose – enhancing security. White hat hackers provide detailed reports on vulnerabilities they discover, along with recommended steps to secure the network further.

GRAY HAT HACKERS

Sitting between the white hat and black hat hackers are the gray hat hackers. They lack authorization to access a network, and network owners may remain unaware of their presence. However, these individuals typically do not have malicious intentions. Instead, they seek out vulnerabilities and inform network administrators or owners to help them secure their systems.

In this guidebook, we primarily focus on the role of a white hat hacker, emphasizing the importance of safeguarding networks while also providing a foundation in hacking techniques. Whether you choose to be a white hat or black hat hacker, the methods involved remain relatively consistent. The key distinction lies in your intentions – whether you aim to protect systems or exploit vulnerabilities for personal gain. We emphasize that illegal black hat hacking is not condoned, and our focus here is solely on the principles and practices of white hat hacking.

What Qualifies as Ethical Hacking?

It's essential to ensure that the hacking activities we engage in are categorized as ethical hacking. While black hat hacking and ethical hacking share many similarities, certain guidelines must be followed to distinguish between the two and ensure the work is ethical.

The primary differentiator between these two forms of hacking lies in the motivations driving the actions taken. Black hat hackers are motivated by power, financial gain, and personal advancement, often seeking to fulfill their self-serving interests. In contrast, white hat hackers, also known as ethical hackers, are driven by a desire to protect their own or their organization's information and data.

So, what criteria must hacking meet to be considered ethical? Ethical hacking follows specific rules:

1. **Explicit Permission:** To conduct ethical hacking, there must be clear and express permission granted to access the network. Often, this permission is documented in writing, ensuring that all parties are aligned regarding the scope and limitations of the hacking activity. When working on one's own network, written permission is not required.

2. **Respect for Privacy:** Ethical hackers must respect the privacy of the network's owner. They should maintain the confidentiality of vulnerabilities discovered and share this information solely with the relevant company or individual, refraining from publicly disclosing network weaknesses.

3. **Complete Work:** Once the hacking task is completed, all actions and vulnerabilities discovered during the

process should be diligently closed out. This ensures that no open doors or potential vulnerabilities are left for exploitation in the future.

4. **Communication with Developers:** If vulnerabilities are identified within the network, ethical hackers should promptly notify software developers or hardware manufacturers responsible for the products in use. This is especially crucial when the company is unaware of these vulnerabilities.

Upon completing the penetration test and related tasks, ethical hackers should share the findings with the network owner. They should provide detailed information about vulnerabilities and discuss potential measures to reduce or eliminate them, enhancing the network's security.

The term "ethical hacker" has faced criticism over time, with some arguing that hacking is hacking, regardless of the actor's motivation. However, the work conducted by ethical hackers plays a pivotal role in enhancing system security for numerous companies. Their effectiveness and success in identifying vulnerabilities and strengthening security measures are evident. Individuals aspiring to become ethical hackers typically adhere to strict rules and regulations, often achieving certification as a Certified Ethical Hacker (CEH) before embarking on their careers.

Understanding Various Types of Hacking

Now that we've delved into the realm of ethical hacking, it's essential to explore the diverse hacking avenues and understand the objectives behind each approach. Hacking comes in various forms, each serving a specific purpose. Here are some common types of hacking:

Website Hacking: When a hacker gains unauthorized access to a website, they essentially take control of the web server and any associated software, including databases and interfaces. Their aim is to manipulate or exploit the web server for their own purposes.

Network Hacking: In network hacking, the hacker collects information about a network using tools like Netstat and Tracert. This type of hacking intends to disrupt network operations and impair its functionality.

Email Hacking: Email hacking involves gaining unauthorized access to an email account and utilizing it to send malicious content such as threats or harmful links without the owner's consent. Caution is necessary when opening emails to avoid falling victim to hackers.

Malware and Viruses: Hackers often create new malware and viruses to compromise the security of systems. Users can inadvertently introduce malware to their systems by clicking on suspicious links or visiting compromised websites. Employing reliable antivirus software is essential to protect your data.

Password Hacking: Password hacking revolves around retrieving secret passwords stored within a system or transmitted by it. Hackers employ various methods to obtain passwords, emphasizing the importance of creating strong and secure passwords as they form a crucial defense against unauthorized access.

Key Loggers: Keyloggers are tools hackers use to record keystrokes on a victim's computer without their knowledge. This data is then sent back to the hacker, who can uncover patterns in usernames and passwords, posing a significant security threat.

Screenshots: Screen capture, another method explored in this guidebook, complements keyloggers. It allows hackers to monitor websites visited by the user, providing insights that can be exploited to their advantage.

Man-in-the-Middle Attack: This type of attack occurs when a hacker convinces network users that they are legitimate. When data is sent from one computer to another, it is intercepted by the hacker, who can either observe the information or manipulate it before forwarding it to its intended recipient.

Computer Hacking: In computer hacking, the hacker steals the computer's ID and password through various hacking techniques to gain unauthorized access to the system.

While there may be concerns that all hackers are the same, it's crucial to differentiate between ethical and unethical hacking. Ethical hackers play a valuable role in enhancing network security and data protection. They help identify vulnerabilities and fortify systems against malicious hackers, ensuring the safety of valuable data.

CHAPTER 13: DOWNLOADING AND UTILIZING KALI LINUX

Now, it's time to proceed with the Kali Linux download process, ensuring that we can fully utilize this system for our purposes. There are several methods available to get Kali Linux onto our systems, enabling us to work with it effectively. If your intention is to use this system for your hacking activities, installing Kali Linux is a crucial step. There are primarily two options to consider: dual-booting with Windows or installing it within a virtualized environment.

Furthermore, we must determine which version of Kali suits our specific needs. "Rumour Kali" stands out as an excellent choice for penetration testing, but keep in mind that various Linux distributions are well-suited for this purpose. Feel free to choose the one that you are most comfortable with at the moment.

SETTING UP DUAL BOOT WITH WINDOWS 10

Our first option for getting the Linux system up and running is to create a dual boot configuration alongside Windows 10.

1. Begin by visiting the Kali Linux website to download the latest version of the ISO file. You can choose between

the 32 or 64-bit version based on your system's specifications.

2. After completing the download, the next step is to create a bootable USB drive. For this, you'll need a utility like Rufus, which helps in the creation of bootable USB flash drives. You can find and install Rufus from its official website.

3. Once Rufus is installed and ready, connect your USB drive to your computer. Ensure that the USB drive has a minimum capacity of 4 GB to accommodate the operating system.

4. Launch Rufus and follow the provided instructions to create the bootable USB drive.

5. In the Rufus interface, confirm that your selected USB drive is recognized.

6. Locate and click on the small CD drive icon below the drive selection to choose the Kali Linux ISO file that you downloaded from the official Kali website.

7. When these steps are completed, click the Start button and wait for the process to finish.

8. Once the process is complete, click the Close button in Rufus to exit the program.

You now have a bootable USB drive with the Kali Linux operating system. In addition to dual booting alongside Windows, you can also use it to run Kali as a live system without the need for installation. Keep in mind that using Kali as a live system comes with certain limitations on functionality and features.

CREATING A SEPARATE PARTITION FOR KALI LINUX INSTALLATION

After completing the initial preparations, it's time to set up a dedicated partition for the Kali Linux installation. Here are the steps:

1. Open the Disk Management settings or access the command line in Windows and run the "diskmgmt.msc" command.

2. In the Disk Management window, create a new partition with a minimum size of 15 to 20 GB by shrinking an existing volume. For example, you can create a partition of around 17 GB.

3. With this partition created, the preliminary setup steps are now complete. You have downloaded the Kali Linux ISO, created a bootable USB drive, and established a dedicated partition for Kali Linux.

Before proceeding further, it's essential to disable Secure Boot and Fast Boot options in your computer's BIOS settings. These settings are typically accessed by restarting your device and entering the boot manager. Please note that the naming and location of these settings may vary depending on your computer's brand.

Once these settings are configured, you'll have the option to boot from the USB drive. In this menu, select the option for booting from USB, which may be named differently depending on your computer's brand.

At this point, you'll see the Kali Linux installation window. You'll be presented with several installation options.

During the installation, you'll go through several configuration steps to ensure everything is set up as you prefer. These include selecting your language, country, keyboard layout, IP configuration (manual or automatic), and choosing a hostname (similar to a username).

Next, set a password for the root user and click "Continue."

For partitioning, select the option to manually choose the partitioning method and carefully select the partition you created earlier for the Kali Linux installation.

You can then choose to delete the partition. Afterward, you'll see the Kali installation partition listed as free space.

You can also select the option to have all files in one partition, which is recommended for new users.

Lastly, choose "Finish partitioning and write changes to the disk." At this point, you'll be prompted for permission to write the changes to the disk. Select "Yes."

The installation process for Kali Linux will commence, taking approximately ten to fifteen minutes to complete. When you reach about halfway through the installation, you'll be prompted about a network mirror; it's usually best to choose "No" for this.

Subsequently, install the GRUB boot loader by selecting "Yes." When asked where to install the Kali GRUB boot loader, choose the second option, which is the hard disk. This ensures proper boot menu functionality for selecting operating systems during startup.

After completing the installation process, choose "Continue" when prompted. Eject the USB drive used for the installation and restart your system.

During the startup process, you'll encounter the GRUB Loader for Kali Linux. From there, you can select "Kali GNU/Linux" to boot into the new operating system. To boot into Windows 10, choose "Windows Recovery Environment" as desired.

INSTALLING KALI LINUX USING VIRTUALBOX

In some scenarios, setting up a dual boot for Kali Linux might not be the most suitable option. This could be due to limited space or computing power on your system, or if you encounter issues that make dual booting impractical. In such cases, you can opt to install Kali Linux within a VirtualBox, offering several advantages:

1. Ability to run multiple operating systems simultaneously.

2. Convenient management of your operating system, including installations, backups, rollbacks, and restores.

3. Enhanced resource allocation control without complications.

4. Portability – you can transfer your VirtualBox to different machines.

147

5. Quick and easy system snapshots and rollbacks.

6. Learning opportunities through troubleshooting.

7. Ideal for experimentation and testing.

However, running Kali on a VirtualBox does have some drawbacks. Performance may be lower compared to other options, GPU acceleration might not work, and issues can arise with USB wireless cards. Some users may prefer regular rollbacks over troubleshooting, and it might not provide the same level of comfort with real machine installations.

The installation process of Kali Linux within a VirtualBox can be tailored to your preferences, offering both simplicity and complexity. Here are the basic steps for setting up this operating system on a virtual machine:

1. Create a new virtual disk for the Virtual Machine.

2. Once these initial setup steps are completed, you'll need to modify VirtualBox settings accordingly.

3. Load the Kali ISO into the VirtualBox to start the installation process.

4. During this process, you'll provide initial information such as location and time zone.

5. Follow the same partitioning steps you would for a dual boot with Windows.

6. After finalizing the installation, you can run Kali Linux within the VirtualBox.

7. Optionally, you can add VirtualBox Guest Additions packages to customize your setup further.

These methods are commonly used when dealing with Kali Linux for hacking and other complex tasks. By learning how to install Kali Linux within a VirtualBox, you'll be well-prepared to tackle hacking and more advanced activities in the future.

CHAPTER 14: WORKBOOK: NETWORKING FUNDAMENTALS

Welcome to Chapter 14! In this chapter, we will explore essential networking concepts and terminology that are fundamental to understanding how data is transmitted across networks. Whether you are new to networking or looking to reinforce your knowledge, this chapter will provide you with a solid foundation.

Section 1: Networking Basics

Lesson 1: What is Networking?

Networking is the practice of connecting and communicating between various computing devices to share resources, information, and services. It enables us to access the internet, share files, and run applications.

Quiz 1:

1. What is networking?

2. Why is networking important in the modern world?

Answers:

1. Networking is the practice of connecting and communicating between various computing devices to share resources, information, and services.

2. Networking is important as it enables access to the internet, file sharing, and running applications, making it a vital part of our interconnected world.

Lesson 2: Types of Networks

There are various types of networks, including Local Area Networks (LANs), Wide Area Networks (WANs), and the internet. LANs connect devices within a limited area, while WANs connect devices over a large geographical area.

Quiz 2:

1. What is the primary difference between LANs and WANs?

Answers:

1. LANs connect devices within a limited area, whereas WANs connect devices over a large geographical area.

Section 2: Network Devices

Lesson 3: Network Devices

Networks consist of various devices like routers, switches, and modems. Each device serves a specific purpose in facilitating communication between computers.

Quiz 3:

1. Name three common network devices.

2. What is the role of a router in a network?

Answers:

1. Common network devices include routers, switches, and modems.

2. A router directs data packets between networks, ensuring data reaches its intended destination.

Section 3: Network Protocols

Lesson 4: Network Protocols

Network protocols are a set of rules and conventions that govern how data is transmitted across networks. Examples include TCP/IP, HTTP, and FTP.

Quiz 4:

1. What are network protocols?

2. Give an example of a network protocol.

Answers:

1. Network protocols are sets of rules and conventions that dictate how data is transmitted across networks.

2. TCP/IP is an example of a network protocol.

Lesson 5: The OSI Model

The OSI model is a conceptual framework used to understand network protocols and their functions, divided into seven layers.

Quiz 5:

1. What does the OSI model stand for?

2. How many layers are in the OSI model, and can you name them?

Answers:

1. The OSI model stands for Open Systems Interconnection model.

2. The OSI model consists of seven layers, including the Physical, Data Link, Network, Transport, Session, Presentation, and Application layers.

Section 4: IP Addresses

Lesson 6: IP Addresses

IP addresses are numerical labels assigned to devices on a network to identify them and facilitate data routing.

Quiz 6:

1. What is an IP address?

2. What are the two types of IP addresses, and how do they differ?

Answers:

1. An IP address is a numerical label assigned to devices on a network to identify and route data.

2. The two types of IP addresses are IPv4 (32-bit) and IPv6 (128-bit).

Section 5: Networking Security

Lesson 7: Network Security

Network security is crucial for protecting data from unauthorized access and threats. It includes practices such as firewalls, encryption, and regular updates.

Quiz 7:

1. Why is network security important?

2. Name one network security practice.

Answers:

1. Network security is vital to protect data from unauthorized access and threats, ensuring the integrity and confidentiality of information.

2. One network security practice is the use of firewalls to control incoming and outgoing network traffic.

This concludes Chapter 14 of our Networking Fundamentals workbook. Networking is an integral part of modern computing, and understanding these fundamental concepts will help you navigate the world of information technology. Continue practicing and expanding your knowledge to become a proficient network user or administrator.

CONCLUSION

The Journey Continues

As we conclude this guide on ethical hacking, it's important to recognize that the journey is far from over. Here, we will explore two key aspects that will keep your journey in ethical hacking exciting and rewarding.

1. Lifelong Learning in Ethical Hacking

Ethical hacking is a dynamic field, constantly evolving alongside technology and the ever-present threats in the digital landscape. To remain effective and relevant as an ethical hacker, you must commit to lifelong learning. Here are some principles to guide your journey:

- **Stay Informed:** Keep yourself up-to-date with the latest cybersecurity trends, vulnerabilities, and emerging technologies. Subscribe to cybersecurity news outlets, follow influential security experts, and participate in forums and communities dedicated to ethical hacking.

- **Certifications and Training:** Pursuing ethical hacking certifications like Certified Ethical Hacker (CEH) or Certified Information Systems Security Professional

(CISSP) can validate your expertise and open doors to advanced opportunities. Consider enrolling in cybersecurity courses and workshops to acquire new skills.

- **Hands-On Practice:** Ethical hacking is a practical discipline. Continuously practice your skills in controlled environments, such as virtual labs or ethical hacking competitions. Real-world experience is invaluable.

- **Ethical Dilemmas:** As an ethical hacker, you may encounter ethical dilemmas. Continuously refine your moral compass and ensure that you uphold high ethical standards. Engage in discussions about responsible hacking practices and ethics with peers.

2. Resources and Future Pathways

As you journey further into ethical hacking, you'll discover a wealth of resources and diverse pathways to explore. Here are some avenues to consider:

- **Specialization:** Ethical hacking is a broad field with many specializations, including web application security, network security, penetration testing, and more.

- **Open Source Tools:** Explore open source ethical hacking tools and frameworks. These free resources can be powerful assets in your arsenal. Many open source projects have vibrant communities that support users with learning and troubleshooting.

- **Collaboration and Networking:** Build a network of fellow ethical hackers, security professionals, and mentors. Collaborative learning and sharing knowledge are crucial in this field. Consider joining ethical hacking forums, local meetups, or virtual communities.

- **Bug Bounty Programs:** Many organizations run bug bounty programs where ethical hackers can earn rewards for discovering and responsibly disclosing vulnerabilities. Participating in these programs can provide both financial benefits and valuable experience.

- **Contributions to Security:** Beyond penetration testing, you can contribute to the security community by conducting research, publishing white papers, and sharing your insights. This not only enhances your reputation but also advances the collective knowledge of the field.

In conclusion, ethical hacking is a journey that demands continuous growth and adaptation. By embracing lifelong learning, refining your ethical compass, and exploring various pathways, you can excel in this ever-evolving field. Your contributions to the realm of cybersecurity are essential in safeguarding digital landscapes against threats. So, gear up, stay curious, and let the journey continue with enthusiasm and purpose.

www.ingramcontent.com/pod-product-compliance
Lightning Source LLC
LaVergne TN
LVHW051240050326
832903LV00028B/2494